Life in the Slow Lane

Tales of
COVERED BRIDGES
written by and for
the people who love 'em.

Jack Westhead

The Bridge Builder

An old man, going a lone highway,
Came at the evening, cold and gray,
To a chasm, vast and deep and wide,
Through which was flowing a sullen tide.
The old man crossed in the twilight dim,
The sullen stream had no fears for him;
But he turned when safe on the other side
And built a bridge to span the tide.

"Old man," said a fellow pilgrim near,
"You are wasting strength with building here.
Your journey will end with the ending day,
You never again must pass this way.
You have crossed the chasm, deep and wide—
Why build you the bridge at the eventide?"

The builder lifted his old gray head:
"Good friend, in the path I have come," he said,
"There followeth after me today,
A youth whose feet must pass this way.
This chasm that has been naught to me
To that fair-haired youth may a pitfall be.
He, too, must cross in the twilight dim;
Good friend, I am building the bridge for him."

—*Will Allen Dromgoole*

Editor: Jerry Wiebel
Associate Editors: Paula Wiebel, Kristine Krueger
Art Director: Bonnie Ziolecki
Production Assistants: Ellen Lloyd, Claudia Wardius
Photo Coordinator: Trudi Bellin
Photo Assistant: Mary Ann Koebernik
Publisher: Roy J. Reiman

Country Books

Front Cover Photo: Jack Westhead
Bridge at the Green, West Arlington, Vermont

Back Cover Photo: Jerry and Barbara Jividen

This Page: Carl A. Stimac
Muller/Doyle Road Covered Bridge, Ashtabula County, Ohio

Contents

For additional copies of this book or information about other books, calendars and magazines, write to: Country Books, P.O. Box 990, Greendale WI 53129. **Credit card orders, call toll-free 1-800/558-1013.**

"I'M A COVERED BRIDGE NUT," admits Pete Calos of Hopewell, Virginia, who shared this photo of the Rupert Bridge in Columbia County, Pennsylvania. It's covered bridge lovers like Pete who shared great stories and photos to make this book a reality.

Why Were Covered Bridges Covered?

To provide shelter during a storm? To calm horses as they crossed the water?
To enhance the countryside? We wondered, too...until the
people who helped write this book provided some fascinating answers.

DID you ever wonder just *why* early-day Americans covered covered bridges?

We did. After all, when you consider how frugal most folks were back in the days when these grand old structures were built over a century ago, the cost of putting a roof and sides on these spans added considerable time and expense.

So why did they "build a barn over a bridge"?

That question continued to intrigue us as we set out to publish this book about covered bridges. And so, as we began gathering memories and pho-

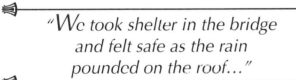

"We took shelter in the bridge
and felt safe as the rain
pounded on the roof..."

tos from the readers of *Country, Farm & Ranch Living, Country Woman* and *Reminisce*, we also sought their opinions on the possible reasons:

"Was it to offer travelers some respite during a thunderstorm?" Hardly, we learned. When you think about it, one of the *last* places you'd want to be parked during a storm would be over a rain-swollen stream while the wind whipped the water into a frenzy.

Yet, while that wasn't one of the main reasons for covering bridges, Jeffrey Reichard of Montandon, Pennsylvania recalls a time when the Rishel Covered Bridge near Chillisquaque did serve that purpose.

"When I was a teenager, a friend and I went fishing near the bridge when a strong thunderstorm blew up unexpectedly," Jeff wrote (see his full story on page 22). "We took shelter within the friendly confines of the bridge. As the rain pounded on the roof and the wind blew fiercely, we felt quite safe inside."

"Was it to protect the span from snow and ice?" No, that wasn't it, either, even though a lot of "guessers" thought that was the reason bridges were covered—to keep the bridge floor from getting slick in winter months.

On the contrary, Penny Silvius from Fresno, California recalls her grandfather back in Iowa telling how he used to haul snow *onto* the covered bridge next to his farm (page 115) so that people could cross with horse-drawn sleighs.

"Were they built for cosmetic reasons?"

There's no doubt that covered bridges "prettied up" any neighborhood. They still offer that benefit—you'll find plenty of photo evidence of that fact on the following pages.

But while the scenic aspects may be the main reason a few new ones are built today, that likely provided little or no incentive to our frugal pioneers.

"Was it to make horses comfortable when crossing the bridge?" You're getting closer. Some horses tended to become skittish at the sight of an open bridge and refused to enter it. Making the bridge look more like a barn convinced many horses to cross over the water.

But it had the opposite effect on a few. Patricia Dupree of Manchester Center, Vermont remembers when her mare absolutely refused to cross the Chiselville Covered Bridge near her home (page 89).

"My husband finally blindfolded her by wrapping his jacket around her head, turned her around a few times so she didn't know where she was, then walked her through."

"Was it to protect the trusses from weather?" Now you got it! Of all the reasons for covering covered bridges, we learned this was the main one—to protect the heavy trusses and timbers that formed the base of the bridge.

These massive wooden beams were expensive and hard to come by. So it was far less costly to occasionally replace roof shingles and rotting side boards ↩

THESE wooden pegs called "trunnels", photographed by Linda Hanson of Cumberland, Rhode Island, show the craftsmanship that went into covered bridges.

of the structure protecting them than to replace the sturdy trusses below. A testimony to how well this worked is the approximately 870 authentic, original covered bridges still standing today.

"Were Some of Them *Really* Haunted?" You'll likely chuckle as you read the "haunting" memories of some who contributed to this book.

While the haunting may be questionable, pranksters did sometimes scare the dickens out of unsuspecting passersby on spooky Halloween nights. And there's plenty of evidence here that the dark corner

---

"This bridge was built by two brothers as a symbol of love between our families. May it always be crossed in that spirit..."

---

of a covered bridge was a convenient place for Grandpa to steal a kiss from Grandma back in the days when they were courtin'.

It's no wonder covered bridges earned the nickname of "kissing bridges". You're sure to enjoy the warm memories of our subscribers in the chapters on "Kissing and Telling" and "Haunted Memories".

In all, there are nearly 200 personal stories in this book, as well as photos of more than 200 different covered bridges. Most of these pictures were "loaned" to us from the family albums of Reiman Publications' subscribers.

Want to visit any of these bridges? There's a complete guide on pages 153-161 that shows the location of hundreds of covered bridges in 29 states and Canada as well.

Finally, we were amazed at the number of people who wrote to tell us they're carrying on the tradition by building their own covered bridges.

For instance, brothers Jeff and Stuart Davis of Westfield, Illinois built a covered bridge across a stream between their homes (page 133). When the bridge was completed, they held a dedication ceremony and hung a plaque on it.

An excerpt from the plaque reads: "This bridge was built by two brothers as a symbol of love between our families. May it always be crossed in that spirit."

When you think about it, that's the best reason of all for building a covered bridge.

REFLECTING life in the slow lane is this photo of the Narrows Covered Bridge in Parke County, Indiana taken by Barb Srock of Deckerville, Michigan.

Standing the Test of Time...

As we compiled this book, we marveled at the amazing strength of covered bridges—and how they've been able to stand the test of time. For example, the Burr Arch trusses above, photographed by Karen Spencer of Barlow, Ohio, have supported the 87-foot Diehl/Turner Covered Bridge in Bedford County, Pennsylvania since 1892.

Many other covered bridges span streams over 100 feet wide without any supports. The longest single-span covered bridge is the Bleinheim Covered Bridge of North Bleinheim, New York, featured on page 71. It's an astounding 228 feet long and has been standing since 1855.

Just supporting their own weight might seem to be an engineering miracle. In addition, covered bridges have carried the weight of horses and buggies, wagons loaded with freight, even automobiles and trucks, year after year.

Part of this strength is attributable to the unique truss systems that bridge builders designed to disperse the weight throughout the bridge. Superior craftsmanship by the bridge builders was another factor.

So was the excellent quality wood they used. Milton Graton, in his book *The Last of the Covered Bridge Builders*, maintains the wood from virgin forests used to build covered bridges 150 years ago was much stronger than the wood we're accustomed to using today.

Northern spruce, for instance, grew much slower back then because timber stands were so thick. Due to competition for sunlight, a tree most likely only reached a diameter of 6 inches during its first 50 years of life. A tree large enough to yield bridge timbers may have been 125 to 150 years old.

This slow growth resulted in much denser, stronger wood. Also, there were fewer knots since there was too little light at the lower levels of these forests to support the growth of branches. Instead, trees had to shoot straight up to compete for sunlight.

May these timbers stand many more years!

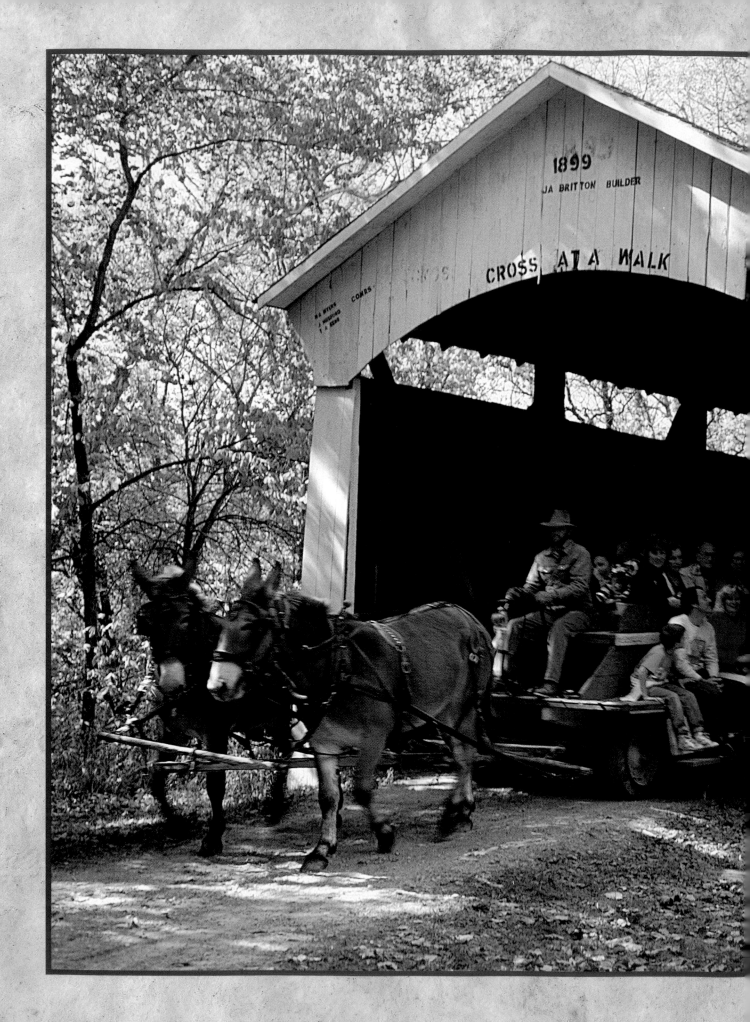

Chapter One

Childhood Memories

*Join us for a trip
to yesteryear...
and some childhood
recollections of
growing up near
covered bridges.*

IOWA'S Roseman Covered Bridge became a world-wide attraction after it was featured in the movie *Bridges of Madison County*. Bernard Booth of El Paso, Texas traveled to Iowa to snap this photo.

The Roseman Bridge Is Named After My Great-Great-Grandpa

By Karen Martens, Foley, Minnesota

When I was about 9, my family and I traveled from Minnesota to Madison County, Iowa to visit my grandparents...and the Roseman Covered Bridge.

I was completely taken with that bridge. I'd heard about it my entire life, and there I was, actually walking on it—where people had walked across it for 70 years before me.

My great-great-grandfather, Edward Monroe Roseman, owned a farm right next to the bridge. The house he lived in is still standing. Edward housed and fed the men who built that bridge, so they named it after him.

As we left that day, we drove across the bridge—then turned around and drove across it again. I was thrilled. To me, it was one of the greatest wonders in the world.

Someday I hope to return to the Roseman Covered Bridge—this time with my husband and two daughters, so that they, too, might have some special memories of the bridge that "belongs" to our family.

Folks Held Their Breath When the Elephants Crossed the Bridge

By Dena Yokley, Franklin, Tennessee

Grandpa Lark used to tell about the time the circus came to town and had to cross the covered bridge between Meadville and Laclede, Missouri.

There were three elephants traveling with the circus, and everyone was afraid the bridge might not hold their weight. They tried to get the elephants to cross one at a time. But, if you've ever seen elephants at a circus, you know they like to follow each other trunk-to-tail.

They started one elephant across the bridge—but there came the other two following right behind the first! As Grandpa told the story, I could imagine the sight and sound of those three large elephants rumbling across the old covered bridge.

The bridge survived the elephants. But unfortunately, age and years of neglect have taken a toll

THE PROTECTION afforded by covered bridges made them great places to put up community announcements and handbills, like this advertisement for a circus photographed by Elaine Grose of Daphne, Alabama.

since then. The bridge is now under repair...and I hope it will soon stand straight and tall like it was the day the circus came to town.

I Remember Canoeing and Catching Tadpoles Under 'Our Bridge'

By Elaine Henry, Kempton, Pennsylvania

The stone and brick homes adjacent to the Dreibelbis Covered Bridge near Lenhartsville, Pennsylvania have belonged to my ancestors since 1895.

My father and grandfather operated the sawmill across the road as well as the apple butter and ketchup cookery next to the mill. For power, they depended on the water that flows under the bridge in Maidencreek.

Our family has so many fond memories of this bridge that we call it "our bridge". Over the years, we've enjoyed sitting on our front porches and greeting the tourists who stopped by. I remember, too, all the fun times canoeing, ice skating, catching tadpoles and swimming in Maiden-

creek...and all the family picnics we had next to the covered bridge.

My parents have both passed away, and it has become time to put our property up for sale. But in our hearts, the Dreibelbis Covered Bridge will always be ours.

Fitches Covered Bridge Was Our Playground

By Eleanor Palmer Gardner, Hamden, New York

"I LIVE a few hundred feet from Fitches Bridge," notes Katherine Kaufman of Delhi, New York, who took this photo. **"My children, nieces and nephews have enjoyed swimming, fishing and rafting by the bridge. It's especially beautiful in fall, when the leaves begin to turn in the foothills of the Catskill Mountains."**

I consider myself fortunate to have grown up on a beautiful farm in Delaware County, New York—in the Catskill Mountains—less than half a mile from Fitches Covered Bridge.

Our school was located on the other side of the Delaware River. So we crossed the bridge every day in the 1920's going to and from school. Sometimes we walked. Other times, my mother drove us to school with our Shetland pony hitched to a two-wheeled cart. It was so much fun listening to the clip-clop of the pony's hooves on the wooden floor.

There wasn't much traffic...and there was a sign mounted over the bridge entrance that read, "Five Dollar Fine for Anyone Crossing This Bridge Faster Than a Walk." So the bridge became our playground. We'd kneel down and watch the fish, run races through the bridge and climb the huge beams and timbers.

Fitches Bridge is of Town Lattice design, 100 feet long, one lane and single span. The bridge was originally located in the Village of Delhi, but in 1885, it was replaced at that location by an iron span. The original bridge was moved 3 miles up the west branch of the Delaware River to Fitches Crossing.

Marsha Williamson Mohr

My Heart Belongs To the West Union Bridge

By Irene Cory Webster, Clarkston, Michigan

My family lived about a mile from the West Union Covered Bridge (pictured above) in Parke County, Indiana when I was a child. Because of the many memories I have, my heart belongs to that wonderful old bridge.

The West Union Covered Bridge is a two-span bridge. That meant there was space on its timbers to carve twice as many initials, names, hearts and love messages compared to other covered bridges in the county.

We lived next door to one of the two country stores in West Union. Each night the stores came alive when men, young and old, gathered there to relax, argue, discuss, chew and spit. Someone would usually top off the evening with a ghost story.

Some men had to walk across the bridge to get to the store—and back across it in the dark to get home. And since this bridge was twice as long as most, it was also twice as dark!

With the ghost story fresh in their minds, the men would never go home across the bridge alone. What's more, the bridge was so scary at night that many men totally ignored the sign at the entrance of that long bridge which read, "Cross This Bridge at a Walk."

I Used to Fish at the Hogback Bridge

By Glenn Compton, Alhambra, California

I was born in Madison County, Iowa, near the Hogback Covered Bridge. The bridge got its name from a steep hill near the bridge that's shaped like a hog's back.

Back in the 1930's, I spent a lot of time fishing from the riverbank under the bridge—and just listening to the sounds of the birds. On the way to the bridge, I'd cut a pole from a small tree and tie on my fishing line and hook. I probably had a grand total of 15¢ invested in that fishing outfit, but I bet I had more fun than the guy with hundreds of dollars worth of gear today.

Sometimes when the fish weren't biting, I'd crawl under the bridge and go to sleep. If I didn't show up for supper, my folks knew where to find me.

THE HOGBACK BRIDGE crosses the North River in Madison County, Iowa. It's 106 feet long and was built in 1884. This photo was taken by covered bridge enthusiast Barbara Pyke of Denton, Texas.

"I'M 90 years old, but I still remember growing up near the Cutler/Donahue Bridge in Madison County, Iowa like it was yesterday," writes Florence Cutler Hotchkin of Grinnell. "As a child going to country school, I went through this bridge twice a day. My father carved his initials in it when he was a boy. They are still very plain to see."

Thanks to Ardiss Cedarholm of Lincoln, Nebraska for snapping this photo to accompany Florence's childhood memory.

I Was Embarrassed to See My Boyfriend's Initials Next to Mine

MY BROTHER, David, and I played on the covered bridge at Harris, Oregon throughout our childhood.

David was 4 years younger than me. My mother told me that when he was small, she had to rescue him one day after I'd led him onto a beam on the outside of the bridge. He could have fallen a long way to the water and rocks below.

When I was in high school, David and his friend wrote my initials and my boyfriend's initials on the inside wall of the bridge. I didn't appreciate that…especially since this boyfriend wasn't the person I eventually married! You can still see those initials.

David went to work for the county and was responsible for signs and bridges. He always made sure our bridge was well cared for. —*Thelma Dickey Fredonia, Arizona*

We Cut Off Our Pant Legs To Make Swimming Suits

MY FATHER was an auto mechanic during the first part of the Great Depression. Then he lost his business.

We had no money, but my mother and father made sure we had some good times all the same. They packed us into Dad's 1934 Chevy and took us to the site of an old gristmill and a covered bridge on Mingo Creek—a place we lovingly called the "ol' swimming hole". We didn't have swimming suits, so we cut the legs off some pairs of our old pants.

My grandfather passed away 13 years before my birth, so I knew very little about him. But later in life, I learned that his farm was not too far from our swimming hole. He crossed that covered bridge many times on his way to cut timber for his sawmill.

My father's older brother drove the team of horses my grandfather used for hauling the timber. He often told about the time he was hauling lumber across Mingo Creek when a storm came up. That old covered bridge sheltered him for an hour until the storm passed. —*John Matthews, Monongahela, Pennsylvania*

My Brother Thought We Were Driving into a Barn

DURING THE 1930's, my family lived in Sullivan County, Indiana. My dad owned a 1928 Reo truck and hauled anything to earn a few dollars.

There was an oil field near our home, and when I was about 10 years old, Dad was hired to haul a load of oil to the town of Attica. It was a big deal for my younger brother, Max, and me to go with him.

It was getting dark as we neared our destination, and Max and I were napping in the cab of the truck. Max woke up a bit disoriented—then woke me up when he yelled, "Stop, Dad! You're driving into a barn!"

Of course, we weren't really about to hit a barn. Instead, we were driving down a very narrow gravel road through a covered bridge that crossed a creek.

I recently celebrated my 74th birthday. Thanks for giving me this opportunity to share such a fond memory from my childhood. —*Don Sluder Salt Lake City, Utah*

"WOW, what fun we country boys used to have at the Campbell Covered Bridge near Greer, South Carolina," recalls A.T. Stevens of Moore. "In summer, we went skinny-dipping—if there were no girls around. As we got older, we took dates there to do our 'sparking'. Our mothers discouraged us from taking our girlfriends to the bridge at night…and Mom absolutely forbid my sisters from going there."

I Watched for Cars on the Bridge Because Daddy's Brakes Wouldn't Hold!

WE RAISED tomatoes on our Pennsylvania farm in the 1940's and '50's. Daddy owned a 1936 Ford, which he used to pull a wagon loaded high with baskets of tomatoes for delivery to the cannery.

We had to cross the Wabank Covered Bridge in Lancaster County to get to the cannery. The road was steep leading down to the bridge. Daddy would stop at the top of the hill...and from the time when I was about 6 years old, it was my job to walk down to the bridge entrance to see if anyone was coming from the other direction.

If it was clear, I'd motion Daddy, and he would start down the hill and across the bridge. He would pick me up at the far end and we'd continue on to the tomato receiving station.

We did this because the bridge was one lane and Daddy's brakes couldn't stop the momentum of the wagon once he started down the hill. It's a miracle that we never spilled a load of tomatoes!

Another bridge I remember well is the Snively's Mill Covered Bridge (also called the Second Lock Covered Bridge).

We had to cross this bridge on our way to church each Sunday. The floorboards were far enough apart that you could watch the waters of Conestoga Creek flow underneath. That was always very scary—I thought we'd never get to the other end of that bridge. More than once, I prayed for safe passage across it.

—*Esther Mae Nolt*
Newmanstown, Pennsylvania

"THE Ashland Covered Bridge, built in 1870 at Yorklyn, Delaware, is still used today," writes Katie Branca of Hockessin. "Children who walk the woods and fields of the nature center nearby have nicknamed it 'Thunder Bridge' because of the sound that cars make going over the uneven wooden floorboards. Most moms and children leaving the nature center turn around and drive over the bridge a second time just to hear it thunder."

Father Let Us Blow Off Steam On the Covered Bridge

I HAD the good fortunate to grow up in a small town in New Hampshire with four covered bridges.

Father would always honk the car horn, and we were encouraged to yell out the car windows when we crossed these covered bridges. Mom said they did that when she was a child, and we yelled our loudest to carry on the tradition.

Of course, the real reason for the honking and yelling was safety, as most covered bridges were single lane. Father wanted drivers on the other side to know he was coming through. But for my brother, Mike, and me, it felt great to blow off a little steam.

Our covered bridges were community bulletin boards. Notices of town meetings, election flyers and other items of public interest were posted inside. When people passed through, they could catch up on the local news.

The old covered bridges also served as meeting places. Militias would muster at them. Local boys used them as clubhouses—and even played a form of baseball within the bridge's shelter. A crack in the floor made a handy spot to drop a fishing line into the water below.

When I think of heaven, I think of the peaceful times growing up near the covered bridges in my hometown.

—*Bryan Therieau*
Concord, New Hampshire

"WHEN I was about 7 years old and growing up in Chitwood, Oregon, our favorite swimming hole in the river was under the Chitwood Covered Bridge," relates Judy Prindel of Corvallis. "One of the main sports was to swim and bob for marshmallows. Someone on the bank would toss marshmallows into the water, and we'd catch them with our mouths. Hands were not permitted!"

The Old Covered Bridge

A dusty dirt road meanders the ridge,
   Then curves downhill
To an old covered bridge.
   Where I, in my youth,
Spent hours at play;
   Oh, I remember—'tho it were yesterday.

There, hearts of love, I carved on its beams,
   'Twas only yesterday—or so it seems.
'Tho years have passed, and I've grown old,
   Youthful memories begin to unfold.

The ancient planks on its well-worn floor
   Hold volumes of history and secrets galore.
Lovers paused here for a moment of bliss,
   While no one was lookin' to steal a kiss.

Emblazoned with bold graffiti art,
   Initials enclosed
In a crudely drawn heart,
   Etchings of love for all to see,
How feelings of youth mold our destiny.

"Henry loves Gretchen" is painted in red,
   And boldly in blue, "Susie loves Fred".
Initials carved on a hand-hewn plank
   Recall memories of youth when
"Betty loves Frank".

The old covered bridge has endured the years;
   It suffers neglect, but sheds no tears.
'Tho storms have lashed its weather-scarred sides;
Like an old warrior, it steadfastly abides.

     —*Charles Clevenger, New Boston, Ohio*

PhotoDisc, Inc.

We Took Shelter From a Storm At Rishel Bridge

By Jeffrey Reichard, Montandon, Pennsylvania

My older brothers used to take me fishing down by the old Rishel Covered Bridge (pictured above) near Chillisquaque, Pennsylvania.

Later on, when I was a teenager, I went fishing near the bridge with a friend. A strong thunderstorm blew in quite unexpectedly. We took shelter within the friendly confines of the covered bridge. As the rain pounded on the roof and the wind blew fiercely outside, we felt safe.

After the storm had passed, we discovered a large tree had blown down just outside the bridge. Both we and the bridge survived unscathed.

Even before this incident in June of 1972, the bridge was nearly inundated by the floodwaters of Hurricane Agnes. Yet this venerable structure held fast—as it does today, at 167 years of age.

"THE Henninger Farm Bridge in Dauphin County, Pennsylvania is another of my favorite bridges," says Jeffrey . **"On two occasions, I spent the night at the bridge while on bicycle tours of covered bridges."**

"MY FIVE SISTERS and I would ask Daddy to honk his horn so we could hear the echo as we drove through the Bickham Covered Bridge near Indian Lake, Ohio," recalls Joyce Roget of Belle Center. "Once I remember waiting for a mother duck and her ducklings to walk through the bridge before we could drive across. Later on, as teenagers, we'd take the back way to Indian Lake with our friends so we could walk through the bridge, write our names on the walls—and sometimes even sneak a kiss. Now I have sons who've developed the same love and respect for the bridge that I have. I hope it's around long enough so their children can learn to love it, too."

We Spent Our Summer Vacation at a Bridge

By Mary Dufton, Clearfield, Pennsylvania

When I was 7 years old, my family spent a 2-week summer holiday at the Snyder Hotel in the village of McGees Mills, Pennsylvania. The hotel was only about 300 feet from the McGees Mills Covered Bridge (pictured above).

The 116-foot Burr Arch bridge was built in 1873 by Thomas McGee for $175. It's still in use today.

The area surrounding the bridge was unique because of the numerous boulders protruding from the river. Of course, this made a wonderful playground for us children.

Every day, along with the children from the village, my brother, sister and I swam in the river and climbed over the large rocks. Some boys had removed a center board from the side of the bridge so they could jump into the river. We also explored the large wooded area around the village.

It was a summer vacation I'll always remember.

"SWANN Covered Bridge near Cleveland, Alabama is 65 years old and I'm 64," notes Ted Swann (below), now of Morganton, North Carolina. "So you could say the bridge and I grew up together. I lived in the house closest to the bridge, and the bridge was my closest friend."

I Covered My Head When We Crossed the River

MY PARENTS moved from Iowa to Kansas when I was 2 years old. When we returned to Iowa to visit our kinfolk in our open touring car, there was no way we could get to Grandma's without crossing the Missouri River.

I always hid in the backseat with my head covered when we came to the river. How I wish the bridge had been covered—it would have made me feel a lot safer.

I'm 83 years old and still afraid to cross open water. So this isn't a story about a covered bridge, but of a little old lady who loves bridges that are covered!   —*Dorothy Handley, Gladstone, Missouri*

The Older Boys Loved to Scare the Little Kids

AT ONE TIME, there were seven covered bridges in my hometown of Salisbury Center, New York. Today, Salisbury Center has the only surviving covered bridge in Herkimer County.

Growing up near that covered bridge was fun... and a little scary. We had few streetlights and they weren't close enough to light the interior of the bridge. So it was very dark inside.

When we had to go someplace on foot after dark, we'd avoid the covered bridge and take the much longer route over an open bridge made of concrete.

You just never knew when some older boy would be hiding in the rafters of that covered bridge... waiting for some unsuspecting kid like me to come along so he could scare me half to death! Of course, we did the very same thing when we were old enough.

We spent every spare minute playing, fishing and

swimming around the covered bridge. Those times are precious to me, and I give my hometown credit for taking care of this last-remaining treasure.

I've visited bridges in other states. Some are longer, some are wider and some are more attractive. But none have more meaning to me than the remaining one in my hometown.

—*Douglas Barton, Syracuse, New York*

"ONE of my grandfather's favorite memories of the Twin Covered Bridges at Forks, Pennsylvania was when his family would drive a wagon loaded with hay across them," relates Amy Stackhouse of Orangeville. "As a child, he'd ride on top of the bales until the wagon reached the two bridges. He'd climb from the wagon while it was moving and onto the roof of the first bridge, run across it and jump back onto the wagon as it came through. He'd do the same thing when the wagon reached the second bridge."

Thanks to Linda Wiebel of Bloomsburg, Pennsylvania for snapping this photo.

Grandma Let Us Eat Fried Chicken and Apple Pie for Breakfast

MY MOTHER, Bernice Tieman Dreier, recorded this memory of visiting her grandparents in Indiana as a child:

"Some of the happiest times of my life were when Mama would let me go to the country to visit her parents, Jarrett and Susanna Bolin, who lived on a nice farm near Huntingburg, Indiana. There were many tall dogwood trees in front of the house and along the side of the road, which, in season, would bloom with big white blossoms.

"Grandma and Grandpa Bolin had a large family of 12 children. Grandma was a good cook, and we had so much to eat. We'd have fried chicken for breakfast if we wanted, and apple pie, too. There was always a large pitcher of rich, creamy fresh milk on the table along with hot biscuits and freshly churned butter.

"During summertime, we often picked corn and other vegetables, filled the jolt wagon, hitched up the horses and drove into Huntingburg, where we sold the produce.

"One day on the way to town, we saw what I thought was a big house, and Grandpa said we'd stop and visit the people who lived there. (He had a twinkle in his eye when he said it.) But when we drove closer, the house turned out to be a big covered bridge that crossed the Patoka River! I was really surprised, but Grandpa just smiled. We crossed the bridge and went on into Huntingburg."

—*Diane Deputy, Sandy, Utah*

We Marched Through the Bridge Playing "Yankee Doodle Dandy"

NEWTON FALLS, Ohio is a charming little town at the confluence of two branches of the Mahoning River. There's a lovely waterfall in the center of town on the west branch of the river and a covered bridge on one end of town spanning the east branch.

The high school was on the western side of town when I was growing up, but the football field was located on the east side. Thus, each day during the football season, the bridge became a jogging path for the ball players on their way to practice.

Likewise, high school band members crossed the bridge as they headed to the football field to prepare for the weekly halftime show.

Most of my friends, some of my relatives and I played in the band. During the last period of our high school day, we marched back and forth through the bridge to the football field to the tune of *Yankee Doodle Dandy* or to the beat of a drum cadence. We loved it! This became our favorite time of day, and it made band practice more fun.

Years later, the cymbal player, a dear friend now living in Idaho, became an artist. She was commissioned by a mutual friend, the trombonist, to paint a picture of the bridge and to include memories of our band days.

I had a great time visiting the trombonist and seeing the painting displayed in her Ohio home. My greatest thrill was seeing my uncle, the drum major, lead us through the bridge that has such a special place in our hearts.

—*Deane Sharp
Washington, New Jersey*

We Wondered Why This "Barn" Was in the Middle of the Road

THE YEAR was 1925. I was 6 years old, and my parents, two sisters and I were driving from Kansas in a Model T to visit my mother's aunt and uncle in Ohio.

We were running late the evening we were to arrive at my great-aunt's house. It was dark and the dim headlights of the Model T barely lit the dark country road ahead of us.

Somewhere near our destination, a building suddenly appeared in the middle of the road. We were dumfounded! Why did the road abruptly end? And why was this barn in the middle of it?

My folks pondered the situation awhile. Could it be a covered bridge? My parents had heard tell of them—but being from central Kansas, we'd never seen one before.

Slowly we approached the structure in our car. I'll never forget the suspense of going through our first covered bridge. —*Lorene Eby, Newton, Kansas*

"I WAS born in Baltimore, Pennsylvania, a quarter mile from this covered bridge," writes Harold Smith, now of Bedford. "As a child, I caught my first trout near the bridge. There was also a big swimming hole underneath the bridge where all the town kids swam—after diving into the river from the roof. In winter, we'd cover the bridge with snow and sled from a mile-long hill through the bridge and into town. It was quite a ride!"

We Rode the Bobsled Across the Bridge on Christmas Eve

By Eileen Damman Berg, Rochester, Minnesota

$10 FINE FOR DRIVING FASTER THAN A WALK ACROSS THIS BRIDGE

We put our Model T Ford on blocks for the winter when I was a child and traveled the 8 miles from our house to Zumbrota, Minnesota in a horse-drawn bobsled.

I especially remember using the Zumbrota Covered Bridge on Christmas Eve to go to church, because it was always so cold and dark inside the bridge at night. I can still hear the horses' hooves go clip-clop on the frozen bridge floor.

We'd stable our horses in a barn near my grandparents' house and then walk to church two blocks away. After the Christmas program and lunch at Grandpa and Grandma's, we'd bundle up for the long ride home. What fun it was!

The Zumbrota Covered Bridge is Minnesota's only remaining authentic covered bridge. It was built in 1869 along the stagecoach route between St. Paul and Dubuque, Iowa.

When a new bridge was built, the covered bridge was retired in 1932 and moved to the Goodhue County Fairgrounds, where it became the centerpiece of Covered Bridge Park. But in March 1997, it was moved back across the Zumbro River a short distance west of where it originally spanned the water.

It's now used as a bike trail and by children crossing the river to go to school. I'm looking forward to walking across that bridge again someday and reminiscing about those Christmas Eve bobsled rides to church so long ago.

THE Zumbrota Covered Bridge is "back home" again. The 120-foot bridge had been moved to a park after it was retired in 1932. In 1997, it was moved back near the spot where it was originally built across the Zumbro River.

I Can Still Hear Swimmers Splashing Under the Bridge

By Theresa Caples, Jefferson City, Missouri

I remember bird-watching and picking forget-me-nots with my mother near the Spangsville Covered Bridge (pictured above), which spans the Manatawny Creek in southeast Pennsylvania.

During spring and summer, we also picnicked and swam there with my aunt and cousins. During trout season, my brother and I sat on the creek bank with my grandfather. In winter, my grandmother would watch us ice skate. Judging by this photo, the cows liked it, too!

That was many years ago, and I now live nearly 1,000 miles away. But from time to time, my mind drifts back to the Spangsville Covered Bridge to again experience the soft breezes with just a hint of the aroma of a nearby farm, the birds singing in the trees and the cows softly mooing in the pasture.

Listen! Was that the splash and laughter of swimmers in the stream? Can you feel the rush of the cool water...and hear the *clunk, clunk* of the traffic crossing the bridge?

27

Sim Smith Covered Bridge, Parke County, Indiana—Photo: Marsha Williamson Mohr

Covered Bridges
rumbled when cars passed
over their loose planks.

Covered Bridges
raised puffs of dust as bare feet
avoided big nails sticking up.

Covered Bridges
were named for the muscled men
who built them, or for the lively streams
whose beauty they enhanced.

Covered Bridges
kept lovers' forever pledges
and pranksters' graphic art.

Covered Bridges
were a community center
with a swimming hole underneath.

Covered Bridges
were scary with thick dark at night—
like walking through chocolate pudding.

Covered Bridges
were replaced by cold cement strips
that are just part of a road going.

—Lynne Gregory, Scio, Oregon

My Grandkids Toss Pennies from the Bridge I Used to Play on

By Robert Sidle, Bowmansdale, Pennsylvania

My favorite pastime as a young boy was jumping into the old swimming hole from the Bowmansdale Covered Bridge, which spanned the Yellow Breeches Creek at Bowmansdale, Pennsylvania. I spent so many hours fishing for trout from that bridge.

After the road was rerouted, the bridge was torn down piece by piece, and the parts were numbered. The trucks passed my house as they transported the bridge to be reassembled a mile upstream at Messiah College in Grantham. There, it connects the campus to the athletic fields.

As an employee of Messiah College, I can reminisce and enjoy the bridge (pictured above) every day. What's even better is that my children and grandchildren can share it with me as I tell them of my childhood adventures at the bridge.

They are also making their own memories as we attend picnics under its roof…and pause to listen to the rippling water underneath and toss in a penny or two.

RP Photo

29

We Had Bonfires On the Ice Near the Old Bridge

By Evelyn LaMontagne, Thetford Center, Vermont

The covered bridge at Thetford Center, Vermont (pictured below) has been part of my life for 73 years. I lived on the same street as the bridge until I was in my early teens. I still live only 10 minutes away and often walk to the bridge to relax and watch the water flow over the dam.

When I was a little girl, I used to cross the bridge with my mother to visit relatives and neighbors. I remember running because I was afraid someone— or something—would jump out of the darkness.

The bridge seemed especially dark and spooky around Halloween, when it was decorated with toi-

let paper. I felt like I was walking through a haunted house.

As I grew older and braver, my friends and I spent many hours swimming beneath the bridge. In winter, we held skating parties and hot dog and corn roasts with a huge bonfire on the ice near the bridge.

Since the bridge is at the bottom of a hill, my friends and I would get on a long toboggan that held about 10 people. We'd slide down the hill into the bridge, where the wooden floor would bring us to a quick halt.

There was very little traffic to worry about. But if we did see headlights, we had a great deal of fun ditching the toboggan and spilling into a snowbank before we reached the bridge.

After climbing the hill a few times, we'd be ready to head for someone's house to warm up with mugs of hot chocolate.

THE KYMULGA Covered Bridge, in Talladega County, Alabama, was built in 1860 and is 105 feet long. Ruby Henderson of Independence, Missouri shared the photo.

We Played 'Cowboys' On the Bridge While Our Corn Was Ground

By Dorothy Jurgens, Birmingham, Alabama

My family lived on a small farm in rural Alabama in the 1930's, when I was about 5 years old.

In fall, our corn was gathered and piled on a wagon to be taken to a gristmill not far from home. There it was ground into cornmeal. We younger children were always allowed to ride to the mill on that corn wagon.

To get almost any place, whether it was church, school, the general store or the gristmill, we had to cross the Kymulga Covered Bridge. In fact, the gristmill stood alongside the bridge.

As our corn was ground, my younger brothers and I played cowboys on the bridge—running through it, hiding behind the large posts inside the bridge and even galloping our make-believe horses through the shallow water below.

Recently, my husband and I decided to visit Kymulga Covered Bridge again. It took a full day to make the round-trip to and from the bridge... and my heart came full circle as I again saw its splendor. Even the gristmill was still standing— just as it was 60 years ago.

Of course, the old mill is no longer in operation. The bridge is closed to traffic, too. But that didn't matter to me as they brought back a lifetime of beautiful memories.

I Have 15 Summers of Covered Bridge Memories

By Lillian Castelli, Raritan, New Jersey

THE GREEN RIVER Covered Bridge at Green River in Windham County, Vermont was built in 1873 and is 104 feet long. Covered bridge enthusiast Elaine Grose of Daphne, Alabama captured the bridge at its prettiest—when the fall foliage was at peak color.

When I was 4 years old, my parents bought a 3-acre apple orchard near the covered bridge at Green River, Vermont (pictured above). I spent 15 wonderful summers there from 1925 to 1940.

I remember horses pulling wagons loaded with hay rumbling through the bridge. The mailman came through every afternoon...leaving people's mail in their mailboxes attached to the wall inside the bridge.

As children, my girlfriends and I played games in that bridge. When we were older, we swam in the water below.

There's one adventure I'll never forget...when I was 13 and giving two younger kids a ride on my bicycle. We careened down the steep mountain road that led to the bridge and flew right through it. I had no brakes, and the bike finally came to a halt as we started to climb the hill on the other side of the bridge. We were all shaky and very thankful to be unharmed.

We had listened for cars before we started down that mountain road. You could always hear them a mile away. But we hadn't thought about the hay wagons and horses that went through, too.

Sides of the Bridge Disappeared Like Magic

I REMEMBER the special speed limit sign placed at the approach to a covered bridge where I grew up. The vertical boards on the sides of the bridge were spaced in such a way that when you reached the magical speed, the boards blurred, then seemed to disappear. You felt like you were looking right through the side of the bridge to the outside.

My father would start out driving slowly, then accelerate until we hit just the right speed for the boards to disappear. I remember saying over and over, "Let's do it again!"   —Bill Ferguson
Salamanca, New York

Close Your Eyes, Hold Your Breath And Make a Wish!

WHENEVER we rode through a covered bridge while I was growing up in Vermont during the 1930's, we made a wish. We closed our eyes, squeezed a button on our dress and held our breath from the time we entered the bridge until we emerged in order to make our wish come true.
—*Mary Rasmussen, Williams Bay, Wisconsin*

My Brother Fell Through the Ice At Quigley Bridge

I WAS BORN on a farm near the village of Newburg in Cumberland County, Pennsylvania. There were two covered bridges called the Quigley Bridges right next to our house. (One of them is pictured above.) They were built in 1824 and named for the family who owned the farm we lived on.

When my younger brother and sister were quite small, they were sliding a kettle lid back and forth across the ice under one of the bridges.

When it was my sister's turn to slide the lid to the other bank where my brother stood, it didn't go the whole way. So my brother went out to get it and broke through the ice. There he sat with his legs dangling in the water. My sister called our mother, who talked my brother into sliding backward on the ice until he reached safety. After that, there was no more going to the bridge alone!

My husband tells about helping relatives move from one farm to another. His job was to herd the cattle along the roads and through the double bridges. It wasn't an easy job.

Then there was the time in 1930 when a load of potatoes broke through one of the bridges, according to my 90-year-old dad. He also remembers when a coal truck broke through the other bridge in the late 1930's and was hanging by its front wheels from the timbers in the bridge floor.

The bridges were torn down in 1947, and a new bridge was built up the creek a few hundred feet. But the Quigley Bridges still remain in my memories. They brought so much enjoyment to me as a child that I've tried to share them with family and friends by painting them on canvas, saws, slates and milk cans.   —*Martha Reineman, Orrstown, Pennsylvania*

My Cousin Crashed the Caddy Into the Bridge

IN 1934, my cousin Junior returned home from his freshman year in college driving a second-hand jalopy. The sight of that old car made his mother shudder.

At breakfast the next morning, Junior announced his plans to visit friends in town. His mother, who felt more secure in a large car, told him to take the family's big custom-built Cadillac instead of his jalopy.

Within minutes, Junior was home *on foot* with news that the Caddy was stuck on the small wooden bridge that spanned a stream near their Virginia farm.

Junior had opted to bypass the main road and take a shortcut over the backroads and across the wooden bridge. But the bridge wasn't wide enough for the big Caddy, and now its front fenders were wedged into the entrance to the bridge.

In no time at all, a crowd gathered to help extricate the Caddy. A wrong move could have brought down the bridge or plunged the car into the water. So, working with care, the men removed one side of the bridge, and the big car was slowly backed to safety.

Later, when the bridge was whole again, Junior made a second start for town—this time on the highway in his own little car. Some wit had decorated his dashboard with a tape measure and a note which read, "For use before attempting bridge crossings!" —*Sara Hewitt Riola, Lakewood, New Jersey*

The Bridge Kept Us Dry
Waiting for the School Bus

IN THE EARLY 1940's, the high school kids in our area congregated in the Camp Creek Covered Bridge in Lane County, Oregon on cold, wet, foggy mornings. That bridge kept us dry while we waited for the school bus. It was wartime and gas was rationed, so we seldom had alternative transportation to school.

Nowadays, of course, the school bus comes right by the house.

Was I born too soon? I don't think so. The progress this fast-paced generation has made is exciting. But sad to say, we've sacrificed a slower-paced lifestyle to accomplish it. Camp Creek Covered Bridge was torn down in the 1950's.

—*Lynn Petersen, Springfield, Oregon*

'SNO FOOLIN', these three boys were on their way to some big winter fun while crossing the Phillips Covered Bridge in Parke County, Indiana. This 42-foot-long span was built over Big Pond Creek in 1909, giving generations of kids a convenient crossing to their favorite hill.

Jack Westhead

Our Buggy Wheel Got Caught in a Crack

UNTIL 1925, there was a covered bridge on Route 40 between Centerville and Pershing, Indiana (pictured above). I recall it well because the bridge planks were worn, and there were cracks between them wide enough for narrow buggy wheels to get stuck in.

My parents had a two-seated buggy with fringe around the top and one old horse. We'd often take that buggy to visit my aunt who lived west of the bridge.

I used to hide my face in my mother's lap when going through the bridge, hoping that would help keep us from dropping between the bridge planks. But more often than not, it didn't.

We had to pile out of the buggy and lift a wheel out of a crack. We'd let the old horse pull the buggy to the end of the bridge empty...and then we'd all load up again and go on.

I can still remember watching them tear down that bridge when I was 5 years old.

—*Mrs. Paul Carter, Liberty, Indiana*

Scaredy-Cat Screamed
When Bus Crossed the Bridge

I STILL SMILE when I think of the covered bridge just west of the old canal town of Metamora, Indiana. That bridge is no longer there, but my memories of crossing it in a bus on the way to grade school will always remain.

As our school bus began its descent down a steep and winding road, the driver would caution us all to keep quiet so he could concentrate.

At the bottom of the hill, the bus made a sharp right turn to follow the high bank of the stream that loomed below. Then, after a sharp left turn, we were within a few feet of the entrance to the covered bridge.

At this point, the bus driver would sternly warn us again to keep quiet. I believe he was nervous about driving over this old bridge, but his orders to keep quiet made us nervous, too.

Entering the bridge was a dramatic moment. We'd hold our breath and be quiet as we listened to the loose floorboards clatter when the bus rolled over them.

The sides of the bridge were covered, but some of the boards were cracked, split or even missing. This afforded a view of the stream below to those brave enough to look down.

At least one young person would become overwhelmed with the excitement and would let out a scream. This would set off the rest of the children yelling and screaming, too. Then the bus driver would scream at us to keep quiet!

As soon as the bus entered the sunlight at the other end of the bridge, we would all become quiet...then start teasing the scaredy-cat who'd started the bedlam.

—*John Harmon*
Yucca Valley, California

My Daddy's Covered Bridge

By Annetta Jones, Tallahassee, Florida

During summers when I was a little girl living in Pleasantville, New Jersey, my family and I used to visit my grandmother in Coatesville, Pennsylvania. On the way, we always stopped for a picnic lunch at Speakman's Covered Bridge No. 2 (pictured above) in Chester County, Pennsylvania.

My father, Charles Connelly, and his friends used to swim there as boys. In fact, he nearly drowned there. His family also used to have their corn ground at the old gristmill that stood nearby. So we referred to Speakman's Covered Bridge as "My Daddy's Bridge".

I have wonderful memories of wading through the stream, skipping stones, climbing the huge rocks and steep hills covered with ferns and picking bouquets of wildflowers.

I moved away when I got married. But after 20 years, my husband and two teenage girls and I moved to Pennsylvania. So I was able to introduce them to My Daddy's Bridge.

All that's left of the old gristmill is the foundation. But the wildflowers and ferns still thrive. And the bridge still stands firm, unyielding and beckoning.

My family and I live in Florida now. But My Daddy's Bridge remains in my heart as an endearing place that provided fun times and precious memories.

The Kids Went Looking for Snakes— And Found One!

By Genna Murray, Augusta, Kentucky

Lew Kornman Photo

There were no swimming pools in our area of Kentucky in the late 1960's, when our children were teenagers. So I'd take a carload of kids—along with soft drinks, chips and snacks—for a swimming party at the Walcott/White Covered Bridge in Bracken County. My kids still talk about those trips.

I remember one afternoon particularly well. My sons, Dale and Buddy, and a really good friend, Rick Jones, were picking up rocks by the creek looking for snakes. Well, they found one—and it headed straight for them. They started throwing rocks at it to scare it away. But they were more scared than the snake.

When they went to get dressed later, the boys discovered that some of the rocks they'd thrown had hit their clothes. In Rick's pocket was a brand-new Timex watch, and it was broken. But like the popular commercial at that time said, "It took a licking and kept on ticking!"

Kids Called Our Bridge 'The Covered'

By Evelyn Comer, Holton, Indiana

The Otter Creek Bridge (at right), northwest of Holton, Indiana, was called "The Covered" by local kids.

It's located about a half mile from the house where I've lived for the past 51 years. The 20 years before that, I lived about a mile from the bridge.

Over these years, our family has gone swimming and enjoyed many picnics at the bridge. Even today, we seldom have a family get-together at our home without at least part of the family walking to The Covered.

For many years, the creek that flowed under The Covered was the favorite place for local churches to have their "baptizings". My sister and I were baptized there in 1933, when there was still a nice beach nearby. The beach has since washed away.

The Covered served our community faithfully until the age of heavy school buses, wide farm equipment and big trucks. It was bypassed in 1996 by a new concrete bridge.

But the old bridge was completely restored and painted bright red, making it a lovely landmark.

"MY PARENTS used to take me to the Pisgah Covered Bridge in Randolph County, North Carolina when I was a little girl," relates Irene Allred of Asheboro, North Carolina. "They'd let me wade in the water, which was *sooo* cold. Then I would sit on the big rocks in the creek."

Thanks to Ann Thompson of Asheboro for snapping this photo.

35

The Covered Bridge Drew Us Like a Magnet

By John Baker, Aurora, Minnesota

There were only about 25 families living in West Ossipee, New Hampshire, where I grew up in the 1930's. During the summer when we spent most of our time outdoors, the Bearcamp River Covered Bridge on the edge of town drew the kids of our tiny village like a magnet.

Our bridge was about 60 feet long and one lane. There were five or six square window openings cut in each wall and a bench-like shelf just below them. We had one important unwritten law.

Whenever someone saw an approaching car, and especially a truck, he was obliged to holler loudly to alert anyone inside the bridge to jump onto a shelf and avoid becoming roadkill.

Swam in Icy Water

The best swimming hole in the river was at the bridge. It was 100 feet long and reached a depth of about 12 feet. As a bonus, there was a nice sand beach under the eastern end of the bridge.

The bridge provided a makeshift diving platform into the deepest part of the swimming hole. Some of the more courageous boys would jump out the bridge window into the water 15 feet below. I wasn't one of them.

The water was very cold in May and June—and tolerably cold later in summer. But cold water never stopped us from swimming. In fact, I recall three of us taking a very brief dip one April while ice was still floating down the river.

The Bearcamp River was a very good trout stream, and I spent a lot of time fishing from the windows of the bridge. It was especially nice to fish there when it was raining because the old bridge kept me dry. The only drawback was that sometimes a fish would flop off my hook as I hoisted it from the water all the way up to the bridge.

One spring, two huge smallmouth bass came upriver from Ossipee Lake during high water and took up residence in the swimming hole. One weighed 4 pounds—I know because I caught it.

Too Big to Reel in

The bass took a shiner minnow that I was using while fishing from a window in the bridge. It was too big to hoist, and I certainly did not want to lose it. So I had someone hold the pole while another boy and I poled a raft out to the fish and netted it. That was the biggest fish I ever caught.

The covered bridge also served as a jungle gym. It was easy to climb along the arches to reach the rafters. Once there, we had an almost endless array of roof braces to climb through.

It was exciting when a logging truck came rumbling underneath the rafter to which we were

clinging. I'm glad my mother didn't know about it. She would have had a fit!

It has been over 55 years since I left West Ossipee. My parents' home was sold in 1974 following my dad's death. But the covered bridge is still standing. It is closed to vehicular traffic now, but I hear it's still drawing village kids like a magnet.

Illustration: Jim Sibilski

Colemanville Covered Bridge, Lancaster County, Pennsylvania—Photo: Don Shenk

Chapter Two

Kissing and Telling

Covered bridges are often called "kissing bridges". You'll understand why when you read these lighthearted tales of courtin' and sparkin' down by the bridge.

PhotoDisc, Inc.

THIS CHURCH in Stark, New Hamsphire is located just around the corner from the Stark Covered Bridge. That makes it handy if, like in the story below, the pastor and parishioners feel a need to keep an eye open for any sparkin' at the bridge.

The Night a Preacher Raided the Kissing Bridge

By C. Collins, Indianapolis, Indiana

Covered bridges have long been a favorite spot for couples seeking privacy for "spooning".

Unfortunately, the rafters of a covered bridge made an ideal roost for pigeons and starlings, and the amount of bird droppings was unbelievable. Three things were certain—you didn't walk across a bridge bareheaded, you didn't ride across in a buggy with the top down and you *never* looked up without covering your face! (These warnings were doubly important if you had your best girl with you.)

Because of covered bridges' attraction to courting couples, local clergy often branded them as pits of iniquity and pleaded with parents to exercise discipline over their young folks.

Heeding this advice, quite a few concerned fa-
thers would check the tops of their buggies for bird droppings after their dating children returned home!

I know of one clergyman who took it upon himself to eradicate amorous behavior in the covered bridges of his town. One night he charged into one end of a bridge, carrying a torch made from cattails soaked in kerosene. Two buggies were parked inside.

The horses saw the open flame, panicked and bolted in an attempt to get away. The two buggies interlocked wheels and couldn't move. There were no injuries—only hurt pride and bruised egos. You see, the clergyman discovered his own daughter was in one of the buggies with her date...and his son and the boy's girlfriend were in the other!

I Rode to Our Wedding in a Carriage

By Kathy Lesko, Pittsburgh, Pennsylvania

Tree-covered hills surround the charming Ebenezer Covered Bridge at Mingo Creek Park in Washington County, Pennsylvania (pictured at right). It's a great place to have a picnic, wade in the creek—or to have a wedding.

My husband, Bob, and I love the outdoors. So we couldn't think of a more fitting place to be married...surrounded by God's beauty next to the old covered bridge.

A horse-drawn carriage brought me, my father and sister, Karen, to the wedding. It was a thrill to travel over the bridge and hear the sound of the horses' hooves pounding against the worn boards.

Dad escorted me to where Bob and his cousin Pat were waiting with the minister. We exchanged our vows under a big aspen tree with the bridge in the background. It was such a romantic day!

Now we return to the bridge with our two boys to picnic and wade in the creek. It will always be a special place for us.

We Spent a Romantic Holiday Visiting Bridges

By Cheryl Snyder, Reading, Pennsylvania

When my husband-to-be and I were engaged, we spent our first Memorial Day together looking at covered bridges.

He'd already taken me to most of the covered bridges in Berks County, Pennsylvania, where we lived. So we packed a picnic lunch and took a driving tour of the six covered bridges north of us in Lehigh County.

I'd grown up in Texas and had never seen a covered bridge in person before moving to Pennsylvania. That made the day a very special, romantic outing for me.

All of these bridges are over 100 feet long and 100 to 150 years old. What's even more remarkable is that five of the six bridges in the county cross the same stream, the Jordan Creek.

THE BEAUTIFUL Bogert Covered Bridge in Lehigh County, Pennsylvania is 187 feet long and was built in 1841. This photo was snapped by Jamie Harwi of Slatington.

We Visit Our Covered Bridge On Our Anniversary

By Albert Helfrich, Cottage Grove, Oregon

My wife, Margaret, and I have visited about 350 covered bridges around the country. But the one we enjoy most is the Office Covered Bridge near Westfir, Oregon (pictured below). In fact, we return every year—on our anniversary.

Margaret was married to an Army buddy of mine, Ken Walters. She and my late wife, Hazel, exchanged Christmas cards on behalf of our families for 32 years. But Hazel and I had never met Margaret since we lived in Cottage Grove, Oregon, and Ken and Margaret lived clear across the country in Baltimore, Maryland.

Ken passed away in 1992, and I lost Hazel in 1993, after 41 years of marriage. In June of 1994, I traveled to Maryland to visit my daughter and her family. While I was there, I attended a reunion of the Army company that Ken and I belonged to. That's where I met Margaret.

We corresponded, phoned and visited cross-country for about a year. Then, on August 12, 1995, we were married on the Office Covered Bridge. We had a lovely reception in the bridge following the ceremony. Instead of the usual bride and groom atop the wedding cake, our cake was topped with a covered bridge.

The Office Bridge is the longest covered bridge in Oregon, and it's unique because it has a covered walkway separate from the roadway (see inset photo below). But the fact that we exchanged our wedding vows there makes it special for us.

THESE PHOTOS of the Office Bridge were snapped by Jan Lee of Minden, Nevada. The bridge is 180 feet long and was built in 1944. "The red and white trim is especially beautiful and reminds us of our first house," says Jan.

The Covered Bridge

A young man took a giant step
   Beneath this covered bridge,
When he kissed his first true love,
   A lass from Cutter's Ridge.

She'd sneak away from her father's sight
   And run to the young man's side.
The covered bridge was where they'd
   Meet—beneath was where they'd hide.

He was 21, she 17
   When Father gave his consent.
So with the preacher, arm in arm,
   To the covered bridge they went.

At the covered bridge they said good-bye
   In 1941.
The second war to end all wars,
   For us had just begun.

They met again beneath the bridge
   In May of '45.
She thanked God that he was home,
   He was glad to be alive.

The bridge was their favorite place to be,
   For the bridge had touched their hearts.
And in their lives so many times,
   The bridge played different parts.

So now after 70 years,
   The bridge has a final part—
A final place to rest in peace
   For the man and his sweetheart.
      —Wesley Tyson, Texas City, Texas

43

ROMANTIC RIDE in the country led Albert and Mattie Anderson to wed in 1910, says daughter Alfreda Brua, from Northwood, Iowa. Alfreda's parents' photo fit this poem so well that we just had to share it!

Grandpa's Tale of a Covered Bridge

"My dad has had this poem for as long as I can remember," says Karen Redger of Plains, Kansas. "It's one of our favorites."

Why did they cover the bridges
   In the horse-and-buggy day?
Well now, to tell the truth, lad,
   I never did hear them say.

It may have been for protection
   From the rain and winter snows.
It may have been for shelter;
   I suppose nobody knows.

Whatever their intentions,
   When the builders did their part,
Those old-time covered bridges
   Have a warm place in my heart.

'Twas in the spring of '83
   When I was a callow youth,
I was a-courtin' the country belle,
   And, laddie, I'd learned the truth.

She was the only girl I knew
   That I'd ask to be my wife.
But to reach the right out poppin' point—
   I couldn't to save my life!

I was an awkward, bashful lad—
   They were common in those days.
Hitty hadn't encouraged me,
   Bein' trained to proper ways.

We were out one day a-ridin'
    Behind my smart Morgan mare,
When a sudden shower o'er took us,
    But not a whit did I care.

I'd bought me a new umbrella
    A-hopin' for such weather,
It was wide enough to cover two—
    If they sat real close together.

Well, what did the blasted wind do
    But whirl freakishly about?
It hoisted that new umbrella
    And turned it wrong side out!

"Oh, Tom, 'twill ruin my bonnet!"
    Cried Hitty in real distress;
She wore a flowered headgear
    And a full-flounced muslin dress.

"Now don't you worry, Hitty,
    There's shelter over the ridge."
In less than 30 seconds
    We were safe in the covered bridge.

I put my arm around her,
    Feelin' brave and bold and free;
With fervid ardor I blurted,
    "Mary, won't you Hitty me?"

The bridge seemed suddenly rockin',
    I was ill with shame and dread;
I turned my shocked eyes upward—
    A-straddle a beam o'erhead,

Sat my pesky younger brother,
    Laughin' in impish glee!
The rain had caught him out fishin'
    And fate pulled a boner on me!

He told the tale to the neighbors;
    They ragged me until I was sore!
The boys all "Hittied" me plenty,
    'Til a fistfight evened the score.

I shied from meetin' with Hitty
    'Til a letter then filled me with bliss.
She wrote: "I hope you will pardon
    My boldness in writing like this.

"You started to ask me a question
    That day when we fled from the rain.
I often have puzzled and wondered—
    I wish you would ask me again.

"Tommy, why don't you come over,
    When you have an evening to spare.
We'll discuss the matter quite fully;
    There'll be no eavesdroppers there!"

Yes, she's your Grandmother Hitty,
    We've never been tempted to part!
Now you know why old covered bridges
    Hold a warm place in my heart.

                    —*Inella C. Bates*

"OUR DAUGHTER, Lucy, and son-in-law, Marshall Fletcher, met while working in Lancaster, Pennsylvania," explains Mrs. John Fanning of Jackson, Tennessee. "They became fascinated with the area's covered bridges—and heard that kissing on a covered bridge brings good luck. So my husband and I made a tiny covered bridge to connect the two layers of their wedding cake when they got married."

My Girl Threw My Class Ring at Me

THE DAY BRIDGE near Prosperity, Pennsylvania was where my high school sweetheart and I began a wonderful lifelong relationship.

We were going steady in 1950, and she wore my high school ring. On a beautiful November evening, we were double-dating with my buddy and his girl. My buddy and I had decided to give our girlfriends engagement rings that evening. But where should we do it?

As we were driving along, the Day Bridge appeared in the road in front of us. We drove inside and decided this was as good a place as any.

I told my princess that I wanted my high school ring back. She became extremely agitated, ripped it off and threw it at me. That's when I presented her with a diamond engagement ring!

That was 47 years ago. I love my sweetheart as much today as on that wonderful evening in the Day Covered Bridge.   —Robert Newell, Zoar, Ohio

We Smile Every Time We Cross "Our" Bridge

KEN and I were determined to keep our relationship on a friendship basis when we met. Neither one of us felt ready for romance. But as time went on, it was evident that just remaining "good friends" would not be easy.

We enjoyed many day trips into the countryside. On a trip to Pennsylvania, we stumbled across a covered bridge...and something about it called out. We pulled off the road to investigate and found the bridge had a soothing and tranquil effect on us.

We embraced and kissed. In the midst of our bliss, we had the feeling we were being watched. We turned and discovered a black Labrador retriever staring and wagging his tail. It was as though he was saying, "You two make a great couple."

Ken and I were married within months. We bought our own black Lab. And every time we travel back to Pennsylvania, we smile when we pass *our* covered bridge.
                                   —Nancy Wargas
                                   Hauppauge, New York

We'd Toss a Penny and Make a Wish

MY HUSBAND and I were born and raised in Illinois...and before we were married, we frequently visited Long Grove.

To enter this little town, we had to cross a one-lane covered bridge, which we dearly loved. It became our tradition at the end of each visit to Long Grove to spend a quiet moment on the bridge and then toss a penny into the water and make a wish.

On one January visit to Long Grove, I was trying to rush our tradition at the bridge because I was freezing. That's when my husband found the perfect way to warm me up—by asking me to mar-

"MY HUSBAND and I were married on the Weddle Bridge, which was originally built over Thomas Creek in 1937 and relocated to Ames Creek in Sweet Home, Oregon in 1989," writes Adrianne Garber-Bertagna of Anderson, California. "I cannot imagine a more perfect setting for our wedding. We visited the bridge on our first anniversary and hope to return each year."

ry him and spend the rest of my life with him.

We've since moved to Arizona. But when we get back to Illinois, we visit our special bridge. On one visit, we even found the pay phone we'd used to call our family and friends to tell them about our engagement. —*Elizabeth Slutowski, Mesa, Arizona*

tiful sunny day in the country, complete with a horse and buggy to go with the theme of our engagement. I think of that splendid day every time I see a covered bridge. —*Cindy Thomas*
Chesapeake, Virginia

He Dropped to One Knee and Proposed

MY BOYFRIEND and I had been dating for about 4 years when we decided to take a day off work and visit Frankenmuth, Michigan, a tourist town about an hour and a half away.

It was a beautiful summer day...and to get downtown, we had to walk across the Frankenmuth Covered Bridge. I was looking at the ducks in the river below as we were walking along—not really paying attention to my boyfriend. Suddenly, he dropped down on one knee and proposed. I was shocked, but, of course, I said, "Yes!"

There were large cracks between the floorboards of the bridge. When I went to take the engagement ring my future husband was holding, he wouldn't let go. All he could think about was dropping the ring through one of the cracks to the ducks in the water below. —*Debbi Gainor, Bad Axe, Michigan*

"COVERED BRIDGES have a long history of bringing couples together," notes Erma Mason of Alstead, New Hampshire. **"The McDermott Covered Bridge in Langdon also helped a couple make their honeymoon getaway after the marriage ceremony. The newly married couple drove to the bridge, where they'd hidden a second car. They transferred to that car and took off—leaving the other car parked on the bridge. Since the bridge was blocked, no one could follow them!"** *Thanks to Linda Hanson of Cumberland, Rhode Island for snapping this photo for Erma's story.*

A Sad Ending Became Our Happiest Moment

COVERED BRIDGES have had a special place in my heart ever since a memorable day when my boyfriend took me to the movies.

The movie had ended, but the theater was still dark as the credits rolled on the screen. While sitting there, tears streamed down my cheeks as I reflected on the sad ending to *The Bridges of Madison County.*

My boyfriend turned to me and said, "Don't worry. I love you like that, and I'm never leaving you."

I started to cry even harder. That's when he grasped my hand and asked, "Will you marry me?"

At that moment, the credits ended, the music stopped and the lights lit up the theater. What had been such a sad ending to a romantic movie marked the beginning of our happy life together.

We were married the following May—on a beau-

"WE RECEIVED special permission from the county to close the Wimer Covered Bridge for several hours on September 7, 1991 so we could get married there," relates Cheryl Martin-Sund of Rogue River, Oregon. **"We set up chairs just like in a church. The bridge gave us a perfect mix of solemn dignity and outdoor informality—much needed on that 102° day. We felt so close to God and nature, especially when a doe and two fawns crossed right in front of us during the ceremony."**

My Uncle Trained His Horse to Stop On the Bridge

By Helen Wilson, West Alexander, Pennsylvania

We live 2 miles from the Erskine Covered Bridge, south of West Alexander, Pennsylvania (pictured above). Built in 1845, it holds many fond memories for our family.

My uncle first kissed his wife as they crossed the Erskine Bridge in his buggy. "There were lots of interesting things that went on inside the bridge," he used to say with a chuckle. "My horse would stop on the bridge to rest each time we passed through. Of course, I'd trained it to do so!"

My dad used to tell how people would gather in the bridge on rainy days. They'd catch up on the latest community news and talk about planting corn and threshing wheat and oats.

My children and grandchildren rode through the Erskine Bridge on their way to school. In fact, the school bus still crosses it morning and night—giving another generation special memories they'll be able to share with their children and grandchildren.

We Live Near the Bridge Where We Were Married

By Krys Eckelbarger, Roann, Indiana

My husband, Brian, and I can't walk through Indiana's Roann Covered Bridge (pictured below) without pausing at the window where we exchanged our wedding vows in 1994.

Right before we were married, we bought a house in Roann. Both my husband and I were new to the community, but we were charmed by the historic aspects of the town and bridge.

Our house was built in 1872—the same year as the bridge, which is just a stone's throw away. We can even see the bridge from our north windows.

There have been many special events held on the old covered bridge over the years, including parties, pancake breakfasts, field trips and church services. But to the best of our knowledge, we were the first couple to be married on the bridge after it was rebuilt following a fire in 1990.

Charles Was Afraid of Dropping My Ring

By Donna Runnels, Abbot, Maine

My husband, Charles, grew up by the Sunday River/Artist Bridge near Newry, Maine (pictured above). The bridge was built in 1870 and was retired from carrying vehicle traffic long ago. But you can still walk across it.

We chose to be married by the bridge in June of 1984. We were both living in Wisconsin at the time. But Charles' parents were not able to travel, so we held the ceremony in his boyhood hometown, where his parents were still living.

Charles' mother, Helen, did most of the planning for our small wedding because we lived so far away. Sadly, she had a serious stroke 16 days before the wedding, was hospitalized and wasn't able to enjoy the day with us.

The weather was cold and rainy the day of the wedding. Of course, we had the option of holding the ceremony inside the bridge if the rain continued—although Charles worried about dropping my wedding band through the cracks of the floorboards into the rushing water below!

But, as if by magic, the rain stopped for the ceremony...and then started up again as soon as it was over.

There was a very emotional moment at the reception as we unwrapped our wedding gift from Charles' parents. It was a beautiful oil painting of the bridge. We wished so dearly that Helen could have been there to see our reaction to it. It was the perfect keepsake for a wonderful day.

It Was a Small World For Mom and Dad

MY DAD, Sheldon Barkman, was an avid collector of covered bridge information and memorabilia until his death in 1995. He was a contributor to *Topics*, the quarterly publication of the National Society for the Preservation of Covered Bridges. At the time of his death, he'd compiled 30 volumes of covered bridge information, slides and pamphlets.

Dad's favorite story was about how he and his father would drive mules pulling a wagon loaded with meat or produce from their farm to Rockwood, Pennsylvania when he was just a young boy. Next to the store where my granddad traded his produce for merchandise stood a covered bridge.

It was a great treat for Dad to play with the local children on this bridge. Since his younger brother had died at birth and his mother died when he was 7 years old, there were few children around and little time for my dad to play at home.

My mother and her family moved away from Rockwood when she was young. But when she and my dad met years later in another part of the state, they liked to believe that she was one of the young children he'd played with on that bridge.

—Joanna Stutzman, Park Ridge, Illinois

Billie Creek Bridge, Parke County, Indiana—Photo: Jack Westhead

I've always treasured that old piece of wood and have it hanging in our hallway with the framed note. A picture of the old bridge that my mother painted for my father hangs with it.

—Ann Vander Maten, Moorhead, Minnesota

Dad Kept a Board from the Bridge Where He Proposed to Mom

A LOVELY old covered bridge near Chillicothe, Missouri was the scene for a special moment in the lives of my father and mother, LeRoy and Dorothy Charbonneau. On this bridge, my dad proposed marriage to my mom.

From that day until the day my mother died in 1982, Dad carried a piece of that old bridge in the trunk of their car. After my mother died, he gave me the wood.

With it was a note he'd written in 1935—the year before they were married. "Honey, do you remember this?" Dad's note read. "I still have the piece of wood in the back of the car. I looked to see yesterday." He apparently had put the memento in the trunk and forgot about it until rediscovering it sometime later.

It Was Love at First Sight

THERE WAS a romantic beginning to my lifelong love affair with covered bridges.

As a teenager, I was invited by a friend to go visit his cousins near Patoka, Indiana. There was a quaint covered bridge in this town. At one end of the bridge was an old country store and at the other end was a house where a teenage girl named Georgia lived.

For me, it was love at first sight. I never saw Georgia again, but my love for covered bridges continued to grow.

After retiring from the Navy, I found a job as a sales and service representative, which took me all over this beautiful country. I was able to visit many covered bridges.

About 20 years ago, I found myself in the vicinity of Patoka. Naturally I detoured for another visit to the covered bridge. The country store, the bridge and the house were all still standing. But I didn't have the courage to inquire about the young lady.

—Jim Creek, Bull Shoals, Arkansas

"MY FRIEND and I were sitting on the Mechanicsville Covered Bridge in Ohio in August of 1938 when three young men from Cleveland happened along and stopped to talk to us," says Betty Beardslee of Melbourne, Florida. "One of those boys, named Howard, became my husband.

We were married 3 years later and now have four children, seven grandchildren and three great-grandchildren. Here's a picture of us back then and another one taken almost 60 years later. We're thankful both for this bridge and a good life together."

"MY GRANDPARENTS, Oliver Thompson and Emma Bagley, were married on the Jericho Covered Bridge in Maryland on July 17, 1898," relates Jean Sherman of Street. "Grandfather arrived at the bride's house, where the ceremony was going to be performed. But the minister informed him that he could not marry them there because the marriage license was issued for Harford County, and my grandmother lived in Baltimore County. So the wedding party walked down the winding country road to the covered bridge, which spans the Little Gunpowder River between the two counties. They walked to the Harford County side of the bridge and the ceremony was performed."

Thanks to Anna Bush of Street, Maryland for providing this photo of the Jericho Covered Bridge.

The Magic Bridge

In spring rain, we waited while water
   Dripped from leaf to leaf,
The dark rafters sheltering us
   From sudden downpour.
Eldon had just learned to drive,
   And showing off was a must.

It's where, in the damp darkness,
   Eldon stole his first kiss—
I must have blushed and simply
   Looked right down at the floor.
Remembering my mother's warning,
   I whispered,
"Oh, El, we mustn't—it's such a *risk*!"

In summer's heat, we sat along its entrance,
   Hoping for a sunfish bite, dangling bare feet,
Eating slabs of apple buttered bread and
   Pretending bottled soda was rare wine.
A tiny ring sparkled in the sun—
   Eldon laughed at my surprise and claimed,
"You're mine!"

In autumn's crunchy cloak of color,
   The crystal creek held us enchanted.
By the bridge we blushed and laughed,
   Kissed inside its shelter once again.
We startled a barn owl resting there,
   And wedding plans were made.

Its roof dressed in bridal white,
   Winter's latest lacy fashion,
We sleigh-rode to the windless safety of our
   Kissing place, silencing our giggles.
We're too old, we say, to behave this way,
   Now that we are man and wife.

By next winter we paced the floor,
   It does no good—
It's 3 in the morning and babies
   Should be sound asleep.
"Beth," Eldon says to me,
   "Go put on your coat."
So we bundled baby Mary up,
   And stowed her in the Model T.

Our kissing bridge, covered once again in white,
   Worked its spell on Mary, too.
We walked her in the darkness there;
   Soon squeaking boards and cold night air
Put Mary into dreamland's sight.

It's not so barn-red as I remember,
   Our old magic bridge.
As El and I walk hand in hand,
   Its old boards creak,
We laugh, and say it's like our bones.

Mary and her Bill have come
   To see our special place,
And weathered boards don't matter.
   I walk the length, turn around,
And see them kiss—
   They're getting married in September.
          —*Kit Redeker, Davenport, Iowa*

Chapter Three

The Granddaddies

Here are some of the biggest, oldest, newest and grandest covered bridges in North America...plus photos of some of the prettiest you'll ever lay eyes on.

The Cornish-Windsor Covered Bridge

By Karen Tasker Anderson, Ellington, Connecticut

The longest covered bridge still in use in the United States is the Cornish-Windsor Covered Bridge. It's special to me because it was built by my great-great-uncle, James Frederick Tasker.

At 460 feet long, the Cornish-Windsor spans the Connecticut River to connect Windsor, Vermont with Cornish, New Hampshire.

James built the bridge in 1866 from a design by Bela J. Fletcher of Claremont, New Hampshire. James could neither read nor write, but his bridge still stands 132 years later.

The lumber for the bridge was cut on the Tasker farm near Cornish, sawed and milled in Claremont and hauled by wagon to the site. The structure was held together entirely by wooden pegs.

The bridge is the fourth constructed on this particular site. The first bridge, built in 1796, was destroyed by the spring ice flow in 1824, and the second was destroyed by ice in 1849. The third bridge (the first covered bridge) fell victim to the March 1866 flood. It was at this point that my uncle and Bela were chosen to erect yet another bridge.

They built the new bridge 10 feet higher than the previous bridges to elevate it above the floodwaters and ice flows. Nevertheless, the water of the Connecticut River rose high enough in 1927 to flow several inches over the bridge floor.

The bridge was renovated and strengthened in 1954, 1978 and most recently in 1980.

When the bridge was erected in 1866, the toll ranged from 2¢ for a pedestrian to 20¢ for a four-horse carriage. Tolls were discontinued on May 31, 1943.

My great-great-uncle designed and built several other covered bridges in the area in the 1880's. But it's the Cornish-Windsor Bridge that stands as a source of our family pride.

ETHEL NELSON, known as the "Bridge Lady" in Cornish, New Hampshire, took this photo of the Cornish-Windsor Covered Bridge when the Connecticut River was raging.

The Cornish-Windsor is so grand that we thought it deserved a "second look" at other times of the year.

PAUL MYERS of Fostoria, Ohio snapped this photo of the Cornish-Windsor on a peaceful autumn day.

SUMMER SHOTS of the Cornish-Windsor were taken by Nelson Maurer of Albany, New York.

America's Faded Jewels

Only built of the sturdiest timber
From the mightiest, majestic oak;
Proudly hand-hewed and fitted,
By the sweat of common folk.

Covered bridges linked our nation
'Cross rivers, creeks and streams;
And dotted the serene countryside
As America fulfilled her dreams.

Nostalgic structures of weather-worn wood
Have stood the test of time;
And can never be adequately described
Through poetic verse or lyric rhyme.

Through the icy chill of winter,
And each spring's torrential rain,
They carried rural commerce
Never faltering beneath the strain.

The years have passed as swiftly
As the flowing waters below;
Absent are the sounds of yesterday
That seem so long ago.

Missing are prancing hoofbeats
From the carriages on Sunday morn';
Gone is the clamor of the Model T,
When the auto was newly born.

These bridges' burdens are heavier now,
Than ever in the past,
'Cause today the word of progress
Seems to be, the die that's cast.

"The old covered bridge is too narrow;
Let's tear her down before she falls!"
Not to mention the graffiti scars,
Formed by a "harmless" prank;
What sadder fate for a grand old structure,
That we should truly thank.

For the covered bridge is America's
Faded Jewel, and vanishing at a rapid rate;
Please don't miss the nostalgic pleasure,
For tomorrow may be too late.

Just go relax 'neath a covered bridge,
And let Nature soothe your soul;
For reminiscing is a wonderful cure,
When the modern world takes its toll.

—*Steve Good, Circleville, Ohio*

The Humpback Bridge

By Nancy Fisher, Vinton, Virginia

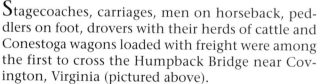

Stagecoaches, carriages, men on horseback, peddlers on foot, drovers with their herds of cattle and Conestoga wagons loaded with freight were among the first to cross the Humpback Bridge near Covington, Virginia (pictured above).

That bridge also felt the tramp of both Blue and Gray soldiers during the Civil War...and many a weary soldier spent the night under its arched roof on his way home from the war.

Built in 1857, the Humpback Bridge is 120 feet long with abutments 100 feet apart. The center of the bridge is about 8 feet higher than the ends, thus giving it a "humpback" appearance.

The bridge was constructed in this manner so that the load is distributed evenly from one end to the other, eliminating the need for a center support. The bridge was built of hand-hewn oak timbers held together with locust pins.

During the mid-1930's, my family rented land next to the bridge. Together with my grandparents, we built several summer cabins. We camped all summer at Humpback Bridge...going barefoot, roaming the beautiful Virginia countryside, living in bathing suits and learning to swim in Dunlap Creek under the bridge.

My father commuted each day to West Virginia Pulp and Paper Co. in Covington, and we'd listen each evening for him to return home. There was a loose plank in the floor of the bridge which made a noise when he drove across it. It was a comforting sound that meant we were all together again.

My mother took us to our home in town each Saturday, where she would bathe us in the tub, wash our hair, polish our shoes and get our clothes ready for Sunday school the following morning. After church, we headed back to our camp by the bridge, discarding our Sunday clothes and shoes as quickly as possible.

It was a wonderful, carefree life for my two sisters and me.

Bath-Haverhill Covered Bridge

By Paul Darling, Woodsville, New Hampshire

Ray Packard

I live 2 miles north of the Bath-Haverhill Covered Bridge (pictured at right), the oldest covered bridge in the nation. Spanning the Ammonoosuc River near Woodsville, New Hampshire, the bridge was planned in 1827 and completed in 1829.

I'm 87 years old and have been crossing this bridge for more than 50 years! During this time, the plank decking has only been replaced once—which shows that covering these bridges to protect them from the elements does work.

In 1998 and '99, a new bridge will be built just below the original one. After 169 years of service, the Bath-Haverhill Bridge will be refurbished, then opened to foot and bicycle traffic and used for functions like flea markets and weddings.

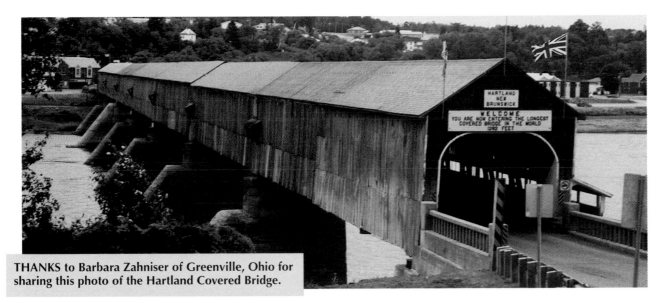

THANKS to Barbara Zahniser of Greenville, Ohio for sharing this photo of the Hartland Covered Bridge.

The Hartland Covered Bridge

By Wilma Outz, Kathleen, Georgia

I was born and raised in a small rural community in New Brunswick, about 8 miles from the town of Hartland. Going to town was quite a trek because we had to go down a steep hill and through a very long bridge—in fact, it's the longest covered bridge in the world.

The Hartland Covered Bridge (pictured above), which spans the St. John River, is 1,282 feet long. It was originally constructed as an uncovered bridge in 1901. River ice destroyed part of the bridge in the spring of 1920. A cover was added in 1922 when the repairs were made.

The speed limit over the bridge is only 20 mph. Vehicles drive across the bridge with their headlights turned on…allowing people coming from the other direction to see them and wait to cross.

A Few of Our Favorite Photos

Enjoy the beauty of covered bridges as seen through the "eyes" of shutterbugs, who snapped these photos of their favorite covered bridges.

"MY HUSBAND and I have been photographing covered bridges for 6 years," writes Barbara Lindberg of Lynnwood, Washington. "This photo of the Jordan Bridge near Stayton, Oregon is one of our favorites. Unfortunately, the bridge burned in 1994, when an electrical short on some Christmas lights started a fire."

"THE CLARKSON Covered Bridge in Cullman County, Alabama was built in 1904 near the site of the Civil War Battle of Hog Mountain," notes James Giddy of Hayden. "The 270-foot bridge was destroyed by a flood in 1921 and rebuilt in 1922."

"CEDAR Covered Bridge is one of the famed bridges of Madison County, Iowa," explains Bill Janke of Omaha, Nebraska. "It's a flat-topped bridge built in 1883 and stretches 77 feet across Cedar Creek."

"WE ENJOY traveling around the country to camp and photograph landscapes and nature," write Blair and Suzette Brumbaugh of York, Pennsylvania. "We snapped a photo of this covered bridge in the White Mountain National Forest in New Hampshire."

"I'VE PHOTOGRAPHED every one of the 105 covered bridges remaining in Ohio," comments Roger Marks of Westerville. "That's a challenge because they aren't as easy to find as, say, a McDonald's! This is a photo I took of the Jacks Hollow Bridge in Perry County on a peaceful winter day."

"THE PRENTISS Bridge near Langdon is the shortest covered bridge in New Hampshire," notes Linda Hanson of Cumberland, Rhode Island. "It's only 36 feet long, but it's still an eye-catcher."

"I'M A MEMBER of the National Society for the Preservation of Covered Bridges and have photographed over 200 bridges in 12 states," shares Elaine Grose of Daphne, Alabama. "I took this photo of the Worrall Covered Bridge in Windham County, Vermont."

"I FOUND the Indian Creek Covered Bridge in Monroe County, West Virginia," says Karen Spencer of Barlow, Ohio. "It's only 51 feet long, but it's sure in a pretty setting."

"I LIKE this photo of the Easley Covered Bridge in Blount County, Alabama because it shows off the Town Lattice truss design, which was one of the most popular trusses used in covered bridges," notes James Giddy of Hayden. "This bridge was built in 1927 and is 96 feet long."

"THE BATH Covered Bridge in Bath, New Hampshire is one of my favorites," exclaims Mikie Lou Fielder of Bono, Arkansas. "Talk about an idyllic community!"

"I TOOK a trip to New England, where I was able to visit a number of covered bridges," writes Shirley Tappero of Black Forest Colorado. "The Creamery Bridge in Brattleboro, Vermont was built in 1879, and it has been beautifully maintained."

"COVERED BRIDGES are more than merely a means of crossing a river—they're pieces of history and works of art," says Hope Bright of Auburn, Illinois. "The Port Royal Bridge in Montgomery County, Tennessee must be one of the prettiest, especially blanketed in snow like it was on the day I took this photo."

"HERE'S another one of my favorite bridge photos," shares Elaine Grose of Daphne, Alabama. "It's of the Cilley Bridge near Tunbridge, Vermont. The bridge was built in 1883 to span a branch of the White River."

"ASHTABULA County, Ohio is famous for its covered bridges," notes Roger Marks of Westerville. "My favorite is the Benetka Road Covered Bridge, which was built in 1900 and is 115 feet long."

"AT ONE TIME, there were 1,500 covered bridges in Pennsylvania," relates Mrs. Homer Keller of Lebanon. "Now there are only 219 remaining, and we've photographed all of them, including the Rosehill/Wenger Bridge in Lancaster County."

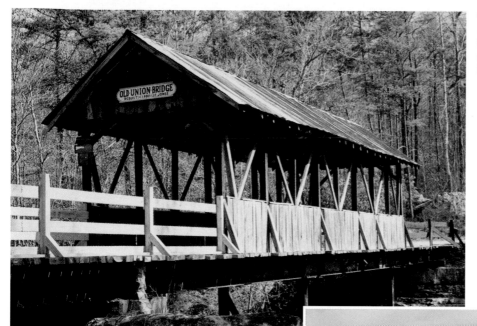

"THE OLD UNION Covered Bridge in De Kalb County, Alabama is one of the prettiest bridges I've ever seen," comments Jesse Ferguson of Irvington.

"I MARRIED a Vermont Yankee," says Evelyn Wilson of Milwaukee, Wisconsin. "So whenever we go there to visit, I ask my husband to take the backroads to look at covered bridges. I snapped this photo of the Gorham Bridge in Rutland County."

"THE DOE RIVER Covered Bridge is the pride and joy of Elizabethton, Tennessee," says Rosa Nieves Gourley of Mountain Home. "The bridge was built in 1882 and has weathered many storms, including the 1901 flood that wiped out most of the other bridges in the region. It's still being used to link the community together."

The Horton Mill Covered Bridge

By James Giddy, Hayden Alabama

The Horton Mill Covered Bridge (pictured above) rises an amazing 70 feet above the water—making it the highest covered bridge in the U.S. It's 220 feet long and the first covered bridge in the South to be named to the National Register of Historic Places.

The bridge is located 5 miles north of Oneonta, Alabama on Highway 75. It's one of four covered bridges in Blount County, which gives the county the distinction of being the Covered Bridge Capital of Alabama.

≈ *I Am the Covered Bridge* ≈

By George St. Georges, South Hadley, Massachusetts

I am the Covered Bridge...a measure of progress in the annals of transportation.

Once I was a mighty monarch—o'er field and forest I did reign...nurtured through years of loving growth as I stretched my arms heavenward. The heat of summer, the cool of fall and spring, the frozen sleep of winter—these tests I've met as nature plied her daily tasks.

Then came the axmen and the artisans. Me they chose for this: an honored role—to make easier the way of the wayfarer...to serve man and beast ...and keep them dry.

I've heard the thunder of hoofbeats, the patter of bare feet scurrying through my mysterious shadows, the joyous splash of those seeking a cool dip below me—or to drop a line into the dancing silent depths, where elusive trout and frog lurk.

My wooden beams have echoed the sound of musket, the laughter of lovers, music of the birds, bray of horse and bark of dog.

And some who lingered left their mark—carved out initials or entwined hearts. Oft have tradesman, circus man, medicine man or public servant papered me with their colorful pleas—foretelling joys—or sale of toys—exhorting all to heed their call.

Mae Scanlan

And history has lived with me; painter and poet I've inspired... composer, too.

And when I earn my reward in Heaven, I'll muse o'er the golden memories of those whom I've sheltered from wind and sun, snow or rain.

Long may I serve. I am the Covered Bridge.

The Philippi Covered Bridge

By Barbara Kelly, Philippi, West Virginia

The historic Philippi Covered Bridge at Philippi, West Virginia (pictured below) was the site of the first land battle of the Civil War.

On June 3, 1861, Union troops led a surprise attack on Confederate troops who were stationed at the bridge and forced them to retreat. Union troops took command of the bridge and used it as a barracks. The victory strengthened the Union position in western Virginia and discouraged secessionist movements.

In researching the history of this wonderful old bridge, I uncovered a fascinating story about its construction contract. The contract was awarded to cabinetmaker and bridge builder Lemuel Chenoweth and his brother Eli in 1850.

Lemuel offered to build a relatively simple structure and made a demonstration model for the committee awarding the contract.

His design drew little attention compared to the more sophisticated models assembled by other bridge builders...until Chenoweth placed his model between two chairs and stood on it to demonstrate its ability to sustain weight. That's how he got the contract.

The Philippi Covered Bridge withstood the ravages of war and floods, but it tragically succumbed to fire in 1989. The bridge was restored, however, to look the way it did during the Civil War.

This two-lane double-barrel structure carries local as well as U.S. Route 250 traffic across the Tygart Valley River. It has the distinction of being the nation's only covered bridge serving a federal highway.

Haralson Mill Covered Bridge

By Lawrence Kaiser, Conyers, Georgia

Rockdale County, Georgia has attempted to rekindle the romanticism and nostalgic charm of covered bridges. We've built what is possibly the youngest covered wooden bridge on a public road in the southeastern United States—if not the entire country.

The ribbon-cutting ceremony for the Haralson Mill Covered Bridge (pictured above) was held in November 1997. The 150-foot-long, two-lane bridge replaces a historic ford that used to cross Mill Rock Creek.

The bridge was made necessary by the development of Big Haynes Reservoir. Mill Rock Creek flows into the reservoir. Until now, the old ford was just a few inches deep and easily passable. But with the impoundment of the reservoir, it will eventually be under 10 to 15 feet of water.

The last covered bridge on a public road in Georgia was built in the late 1890's.

About 100 years later, we chose a covered bridge to blend with the historic setting of Haralson Mill Road and the reservoir. However, I sincerely doubt that a structure of this type and size will ever be built again on a public road in Georgia.

The Blenheim Covered Bridge

By Doris Vrooman, North Blenheim, New York

"THE BLENHEIM Covered Bridge is a National Historic Civil Engineering Landmark," says Richard Wilson of Rome, New York, who took this photo.

The old covered bridge at North Blenheim, New York (pictured above) is the longest single-span covered bridge in the world.

The Blenheim Covered Bridge crosses Schoharie Creek. It boasts trusses 228 feet long and carries a 210-foot clear span.

What makes this engineering feat even more remarkable is that the bridge has two lanes.

Built in 1855, the Blenheim Covered Bridge has a colorful past. Town records show that Hezikiah Dickerman, the Blenheim Bridge Company president, was a prominent member of the local temperance society.

Legend has it that during construction of the bridge, some workers had a jug of "liquid refreshment" on the job one day when Mr. Dickerman arrived. They quickly stuck the jug between the stones of a partially finished abutment.

Mr. Dickerman personally stayed to supervise the completion of that abutment that day. So far as anyone knows, the jug is still entombed there—vintage 1855!

The Roberts Bridge

By Mr. and Mrs. Heber Felton, Lewisburg, Ohio

The Roberts Bridge (at right) is the most cherished of the seven remaining covered bridges in Preble County, Ohio.

Built in 1829 on what is now U.S. Route 127 over Seven Mile Creek, the Roberts Bridge is the oldest double-barreled bridge in Ohio and one of only six remaining in the United States. The term double-barreled means that it was built to accommodate two lanes of traffic.

In 1986, the bridge was badly burned. A group of concerned people assembled at the burned structure shortly after the fire and pledged to restore it. They also raised funds to move the bridge to a more public place where more people could appreciate its uniqueness and beauty. So Roberts Bridge was relocated to the town of Eaton, where it still spans Seven Mile Creek. The dedication of the restored bridge was held in 1991.

BRIDGE ENTHUSIAST Barbara Zahniser of Greenville, Ohio snapped this photo.

THIS POEM underscores the mighty power of the water that is sometimes unleashed against covered bridges—making it all the more remarkable that these magnificent structures have stood so well for so long. The poem was shared by Joanne Kash of Daytona Beach, Florida. It was written by her grandmother, a published New England poet who died in 1970 at the age of 99.

The New Covered Bridge

I think the frozen river laughs
To hear the piles go down—
They're building a new bridge up in
My corner of the town.

It keeps me laughing as it hears
What busy workers say:
"If all the ice up north comes down,
This bridge is bound to stay!
It's higher built…"

…The river says:
"And what is that to me?
I'll have more power for every time
That they have slain a tree,

"In pastures, and in woodlots, and
On each side of my banks,
So water can run free and fast.
I'll heave and lift the planks,

"And carry them as easily
As winds a grain of sand,
Until the wreckage, as before,
Will strew the meadowland."

But all a while above its talk
I hear men driving piles,
And strangers, coming to the place,
Will view the work with smiles,

And bid each other Howdy do?
Good morning! or Good day!
And all agree (the river laughs),
"This bridge is bound to stay!"

73

The Springwater Volunteer Bridge

By Dorothy Wagoner, Wild Rose, Wisconsin

One of the newest covered bridges was built with good old-fashioned volunteerism.

VOLUNTEERS who worked on the Springwater Volunteer Bridge averaged 74 years of age (right). Photos at far right show the work in progress, and the finished result is above.

It all started in 1989, when the old Springwater bridge in the town of Springwater, Wisconsin needed replacing. An engineering firm was hired to design a new bridge of concrete and steel at an estimated cost of $100,000.

About this time, a Springwater town board member, Garth Towne, found himself in Pennsylvania for his daughter's wedding. While he was there, he became intrigued by the area's many covered wooden bridges.

On one of them was a plaque that indicated the bridge was designed and built by Itheil Towne, Garth's great-grandfather's cousin. That gave him the idea of building a covered bridge back home in Springwater instead of the concrete and steel bridge the engineers had proposed.

After many meetings with the Department of Transportation, engineers and representatives from other agencies, the project seemed doomed. For one thing, the Department of Transportation insisted on a two-lane bridge, and the covered bridge was designed for one lane only. To get the bridge they wanted, the Springwater Town Board decided to drop all state and federal funds and build the structure on their own.

The town set up a "Covered Bridge Fund" at a local bank to raise money for the $40,000 bridge. Funding came from a variety of sources, including an anonymous donor who gave T-shirts to sell, which were emblazoned with the logo "Covering the Future with the Past".

Demolition of the old bridge began in July 1996. Great timbers of Douglas fir were hauled in from Oregon in August, and construction began in Garth's pickle shed. The bridge was assembled in the shed, then disassembled so it could be erected at its new location, 1 mile west of Saxeville off County Trunk A, on Covered Bridge Road.

In October, the large trusses were hauled to the site and swung into place by a crane. Rafters were bolted together and the roof set in place before winter. All this was done through donations of labor and equipment.

Construction resumed in the spring of 1997. The average age of the core group of construction volunteers was 74: Lionel Peck, 73, Norman Suranne, 65, Steve Slavik, 73, and Alden Attoe, 86—the ramrod of the crew!

Meanwhile, Kermit Jorgensen and his wife, Shirley, were turning their land next to the bridge into a peaceful little park. They bought a gazebo and picnic table, and had a landscaper add flowers and shrubs and build a concrete walkway, turning what was once a barnyard where Kermit grew up into a beautiful flower garden on the Pine River (see photo at lower right).

The Springwater Volunteer Bridge was dedicated on June 1, 1997 as a place where folks can enjoy the tranquillity of a park setting—with beautiful flowers and plants, the sound of the rippling water from the Pine River and the songs of the birds.

You can feel God's presence at our covered bridge.

Cataract Falls Covered Bridge, Owen County, Indiana—Photo: Jack Westhead

Chapter Four

My Special Bridge

Covered bridge lovers across the country share memories and photos of the bridges most dear to them.

Time Stands Still at the Bridge Where I Was Baptized

By Shirley Bowles, Richardson, Texas

Sandy Creek Covered Bridge in Jefferson County, Missouri (pictured above) is special to me because the most important event of my life took place there during the summer of 1953.

That summer, I attended the Bates Creek Christian Camp and decided to be baptized as a symbol of the conversion I experienced during the camp. The church I attended as a child used Sandy Creek for baptisms. So on a hot August Sunday afternoon, my younger brother, Lloyd, and I and several of our friends joined church members under the covered bridge for the service.

We wore white robes as we waded out into waist-deep water. There we were immersed while the congregation sang *Shall We Gather at the River*. I'll never forget facing the beautiful red covered bridge as I was raised up out of the water.

More than 40 years later, I revisited Sandy Creek Bridge (see top left photo). As I walked down the bank toward the water with my husband, Bill, I heard children running through the bridge—laughing and hollering to create echoes. It brought back childhood memories of when I enjoyed doing the same thing. Even our swimming hole was still there—the same size and still about waist deep.

What's more, the bridge was just as red and beautiful as on that memorable Sunday when I was baptized. Time had stood still in this special place.

The Knox Bridge Helped Me Through Tough Times

By Diane Prusinowski, Conshohocken, Pennsylvania

Two years ago, my family was besieged by tragedy. The Knox Covered Bridge in Valley Forge National Park, Valley Forge, Pennsylvania (pictured above), helped me through those tough times.

In a span of 10 months, I lost my best friend and my mom. My dad, who is a stroke victim, had to move in with me. I also had two surgeries in which my jaw was wired shut.

I love walking through the park. During this difficult time, the Knox Covered Bridge reminded me of stability and happy memories.

I felt that no matter how bad things seemed at the moment, there was a whole new picturesque scene—a new and different perspective—when I walked across that bridge to the other side. It reminded me that happiness is always there. I just may have to look a little harder for it.

I teach and coach field hockey in the fall and lacrosse in the spring. So there are periods when I don't have time for my walks to the bridge. So I commissioned a local artist to paint an oil painting of the Knox Bridge. Now I can escape and find those happy memories and relaxed feelings anytime I need to—right in my own home.

"MY HUSBAND, George, took this photo of the Swiftwater Covered Bridge spanning the Ammonoosuc River at Bath, New Hampshire," writes Beverly Beaman of Webster, New York. "It was built in 1849 as a two-span bridge 158 feet long. It was rebuilt in 1977, and an additional pier was added in 1988."

We Saved the Bridge Near Roy Rogers' Home

By Ruth Ann Evans, Sciotoville, Ohio

I met cowboy movie star Roy Rogers at the Otway Covered Bridge (pictured below) in Otway, Ohio.

Roy grew up just a few miles from the bridge in a place called Duck Run—one of those towns that you'd miss if you blinked while driving through it.

It happened that he was visiting relatives in the area and attending the annual Otway Covered Bridge Festival.

Since childhood, I'd been a big fan of Mr. Rogers, and it was a special treat to meet him in person. He was very pleasant and friendly and talked with me for quite some time.

The Otway Covered Bridge is the only remaining covered bridge in Scioto County, Ohio. It was built in 1874 by the Smith Bridge Company for the unbelievable sum of $14.30 per linear foot. At 127 feet, the bridge cost $1,816.10 to build.

Ohio State Route 348 passed through the bridge across Scioto Brush Creek. But the bridge was bypassed and scheduled for demolition in the early 1960's when the highway was rerouted.

It was only through the diligent efforts of an enterprising group of Otway citizens that the bridge was spared. In fact, that proud old bridge is standing proof that when a group of determined ladies set their minds to a good cause (like Roy Rogers chasing the outlaws), nothing can stand in their way.

Arms got twisted...and things got done! The group formed the Otway Covered Bridge Society and convinced the Ohio Highway Department to deed the bridge to the society.

With community volunteers, donated materials and fund-raisers, the bridge was restored and is maintained with pride for use by the community.

The following poems were written by Rita Smith Balser of Lancaster, Ohio as part of the campaign to save the Otway Covered Bridge:

Witness for the Defense

"I understand there's a trial
The subject of which is me.
Progress vs. sentiment,
What will the verdict be?"

"Now I know that I am just a bridge
And don't quite understand,
But I know from hearing people talk
That something's being planned.

"So if the court pleases, your honor,
And you promise not to laugh,
I'd like to take the witness stand
And speak on my own behalf.

"Lo, many years I've spanned this creek
With timbers wide and long,
And through the rain and wind and sleet
I've held up stout and strong.

"And if sometimes I weakened
Under wheel and foot and hoof,
Some men would come and patch me up
With brand-new floor and roof.

"True, I'm not made of modern steel
With girders high and wide,
But I've got nice dark niches,
Where little boys can hide.

"When Grandpa courted Grandma
And the night was filled with bliss,
The horse would stop beneath my roof
While Grandpa stole a kiss.

"Oh, I could talk forever
Of the things I've heard and seen—
Of swaybacked mules and shiny cars
And all things in between.

"I speak for all my brothers
Tho', alas, we number few;
Please spare my life, your honor,
We've served you well and true.

"For all the covered bridges
To be found yet anyplace
I beg you, sir, for mercy
And I thereby rest my case."

The Verdict

"I've carefully weighed the evidence
Presented here today.
I've deliberated long and hard
On what I have to say.

"As servant of the people,
I'm really duty bound
To keep our roads and highways safe
And keep our bridges sound.

"I must find you 'guilty', bridge,
Of clinging to the past,
And being far too old and frail
For cars that drive too fast.

"But this old judge still has a heart
And quite a memory, too.
So after long and careful thought
Here is my plan for you.

"I sentence you forever
To stand right where you are.
Your floorboards never more will feel
A single passing car.

"The new highway will pass you by
And all the traffic, too,
But travelers and tourists
Will stop and visit you.

"Little boys may carve their names
On each and every rafter.
The noise and mess of picnic crowds
Will haunt you ever after.

"On behalf of all the Grandmas
Who beneath your roof were kissed,
I spare your life with a sigh and a tear and say—
Case closed and court dismissed."

My Bridge Is So Peaceful on Foggy Mornings

By Martha Dougherty, West Alexander, Pennsylvania

I've always considered the Mays Covered Bridge near West Alexander, Pennsylvania "my" covered bridge.

We've lived a half mile from that bridge for the last 40 years. Our three children grew up traveling this bridge, and it has been part of their lives for more than 30 years as well.

The weather was bitter cold on New Year's Day a few years ago. In fact, it had been well below zero for several days. Plus a heavy fog had moved in… and lingered and lingered and lingered. The combination of fog and cold temperatures resulted in a heavy layer of hoarfrost generously coating everything.

On that New Year's Day, my husband and I went for a walk. That was when I took this picture (above) of my bridge in the fog.

Whenever I look at this picture, I can't help but think of the stories my bridge could tell if only it could talk. On this misty morning, perhaps it would say: "The fog is heavy, a bitter cold morning in winter. The scenery appears and disappears as the fog lifts and falls—like a gray blanket, but one that does nothing to warm the air.

"Listen! Do you hear? Horses coming slowly, pulling a heavy load. Their hooves echo through the surrounding fog, sounding eerie in the stillness. You can hear them, but you can't see anything— ghost horses in the fog.

"All at once they appear faintly—shadowy forms in the fog, and as they get closer you can see they're pulling a wagon loaded with hay. Closer and closer they come and finally pass under my roof and continue up the hill, disappearing as the fog closes in once again.

"For another instant, the echo of their hooves lingers in the still air. Then all is quiet, as only a fog-shrouded countryside can be."

We Found All Six Bridges—
Even Though We Got Lost

By Midge Vanausdoll, Pico Rivera, California

Whenever we travel through Oregon, we have to stop in the Cottage Grove area to see the covered bridges.

On our last trip from California to Washington State, we made our usual stop. But we got lost looking for the bridges.

In the end, we found all six covered bridges in the area and photographed them. This one is the Stewart Bridge, built in 1930.

As you can see from this photo, the Oregon scenery is fantastic. So even though we got lost, it was worth the effort.

We Never Saw the Butterflies Before

By John and Mabel Zeiset, East Earl, Pennsylvania

We farmed for years near the Weaver Mill Covered Bridge in Lancaster County, Pennsylvania (pictured at right).

Our children had wonderful times playing in that bridge. Sometimes they hung on the overhead cable and swung across the bridge. But what they liked to do best was watch cars driving through the bridge—hoping to catch couples sneaking a kiss.

Now we've retired from farming and have moved to the other side of the bridge. We love to watch the butterflies that visit when the water gets high. The funny thing is we never saw them on the other side of the bridge!

Kingsbury/Hyde Bridge, East Bethel, Vermont—Photo: Mae Scanlan

I Have So Much to Tell

If I could tell my story,
So many things I could reveal,
My age is hundreds of years,
A body that holds etchings and carvings
Of the past.

Many a horse-drawn carriage
Has traveled through me
On a Sunday afternoon,
Or a wagonload of hay on its way
To the barn.

Many, many nights
I've watched the moon rise
And reflect itself on the water.

I've held nests of tiny bird eggs
In my protection until
They hatched and were able to fly away,
Leaving behind their nests
And a lonely guardian.

My most joyous memories
Were the young lovers making plans
(Thinking they were alone),
And of the children they would have,
Some coming back years later
To show the children
And tell them of the carvings they put there
So long ago.

They are all akin to me, even the muskrat
That thinks he owns the water.

I can still hear *Amazing Grace*
And *Shall We Gather at the River*
As a baptism was held close by me,
And I knew God had gained another soul.

Yes, I'm getting old now
And beginning to feel my age,
My boards are loose and decaying, and
I don't know if there is a heaven
And final resting place for covered bridges.

I have so many memories
And stories I could tell
If I weren't a covered bridge.

I worry now,
Will they do away with me
Because they won't need me anymore?
Can anyone hear me?
I have so much to tell!

—Lucy Nolan, Ashland, Kentucky

Why Did the Chicken Cross The Bridge?

By Pat Cook, Enola, Pennsylvania

I love to visit covered bridges…and these are just *a few* of the photos I've taken of bridges around the country.

One day I went to take pictures of a covered bridge in Chester County, Pennsylvania while my mother sat in the car and waited. I was climbing a steep bank when a chicken came along and started pecking at my ankles.

It followed me onto the bridge, and about that time a car came by. The driver rolled down his window and joked, "Out walking your chicken, I see."

I didn't take a picture of the chicken. That was unfortunate because when I got back to the car, I couldn't convince my mother there had been one on the bridge with me. But a year or two later, I discovered the book *American Covered Bridges*. There on page 76 was a chicken walking in that bridge—and acting like he owned the place!

Perhaps my most memorable visit to a covered bridge was when my mother and I stopped at the Gilpin Covered Bridge in Cecil County, Maryland. When I returned to the car from taking pictures, my mother had the doors locked and the windows rolled up and was yelling something I couldn't understand.

Then I saw what the problem was—a large snake was under my car…with its head at my door and its tail stretched clear on the other side! Mother doesn't drive, so she couldn't move the car. I was trapped outside my own vehicle.

Mother honked the horn while I threw stones. The snake didn't move. Finally I stopped a man and told him my tale. He grabbed a tree branch and got down on his hands and knees to look. No snake.

I jumped in my car and took off…but all the time I was fearful that the snake had crawled into the car and would wrap itself around my legs at any second.

That snake had probably slithered off when he saw the man with the tree branch. But when we got home, I didn't park in the garage—just in case.

I had not encountered a ghost at the bridge that day, but that snake was just as bad!

BUSKIRK Covered Bridge crosses the Hoosic River between Rensselaer and Washington Counties near the town of Buskirk, New York. The bridge was built in 1880 with Howe trusses and is 164 feet long.

"THIS PRETTY little bridge in Bedford County, Pennsylvania is known as the Halls Mill Covered Bridge," shares Pat. **"It's 96 feet long and was built in 1872. Note the Burr Arch truss design."**

"I TRAVELED to Maine to take this photo of the Hemlock Covered Bridge at the old channel of the Saco River near Fryeburg," says Pat. "This bridge was built in 1857 and is 116 feet long."

"A DEDICATION was held June 7, 1997 for the completion of renovation work for the Heirline/Kinton Covered Bridge (below) in Bedford County, Pennsylvania," Pat explains. "The bridge was originally built in 1902 and is 136 feet long."

STAATS MILL CAMP Covered Bridge (above) is located in Jackson County, West Virginia, where it crosses a pond at Cedar Lakes. It was built in 1888 and is 97 feet long.

"THIS BEAUTY is the Saucks Covered Bridge (below) at Gettysburg, Pennsylvania," comments Pat. "It was built in 1854 with the Town Lattice truss design, which is my favorite type of truss."

THE GILPIN Covered Bridge in Cecil County, Maryland is 119 feet long and was built in 1860. "This is where I had a run-in with a snake while I was taking pictures," says Pat.

"THERE IS a lot of history surrounding the Crowley Covered Bridge at Oakland, Oregon," say Bob and Neva Smith of Lacey, Washington. "The bridge's namesake is Martha Leland Crowley, who is buried just north of the bridge. The 14-year-old was a member of the first wagon train to enter Oregon by the Applegate Trail in 1846. The Harkness and Twogood Stage House, built in 1857, stands northeast of the bridge. The 1880 guest register includes the names of President Rutherford B. Hayes and General William T. Sherman."

"MY SISTER, Patti, and I were driving through the countryside when we came across this leaning covered bridge," writes Jacquie Pearson of Kansas City, Missouri. "Patti hammed it up and leaned along with the bridge when I snapped this photo."

Dad Proposed to Mom On the Bridgeton Bridge

THE BRIDGETON BRIDGE in Parke County, Indiana holds a special place in the hearts of our family. It was in this bridge that my father, Carl, stopped the horse and buggy and proposed to my mother, Elizabeth.

I played around this bridge as a small boy and fished with my uncle in Big Raccoon Creek.

My father told me many stories about the Bridgeton Bridge—like the time he and his brothers were camping by the creek when a storm came up. They sought refuge inside the bridge all night.

Dad recorded many of these stories about growing up in Parke County, the covered bridge capital of the world, in an autobiography titled *The Covered Bridge*. —*Gene Killion, Paris, Illinois*

We Pulled Together to Save the Old Bridge

IN JUNE 1972, floodwaters on Conocheague Creek damaged Martin's Mill Covered Bridge near Greencastle, Pennsylvania. A fund-raising drive was launched to restore the 225-foot span.

The following thoughts were shared by G. Fred Ziegler at the rededication of the bridge on June 3, 1973. They underscore the importance of covered bridges to our community:

"Today, in its 124th year, the Martin's Mill Covered Bridge is a reminder of a bygone era. It stands at the foot of steep hills whose rocky banks still nourish wildflowers and whose winding roads were once no more than trails.

"It spans a creek whose Indian name suggests the perils of those early settlers who chose this lonely site as a source of water power. It rests on stones that for a century and a quarter have withstood the currents of the Conocheague.

"It preserves on the sturdy beams of its latticed trusses the names and initials of successive generations. It recalls the clip-clop of the doctor's buggy on its rounds, the rumble of two-horse wagons on their way to the mill, the rattle of rain and sleet as travelers took refuge there, the whisper of lovers in a furtive rendezvous.

"Around it the willows and sycamores lean across the banks, the waters ripple in the sunlight, the bright blue kingfishers dive for their prey, the woodpeckers tap on dead tree trunks, the whippoorwills herald the coming of the night.

"The old bridge stands, too, for something more. Twice doomed and twice reprieved, it is a monument to a community's determination to preserve its heritage, to resist what seemed an irrevocable decision, to salvage what seemed a total loss. It is a tribute to dedicated leadership and enthusiastic response, a lavishing of thousands of dollars in contributions and untold hours of voluntary labor.

"It is a bridge between man's distant past, when nature often seemed to be his enemy, and a future in which his survival depends on his respect for his natural environment.

"Here, remote from the busy highways, to be cherished by us and our descendants, is a place of natural beauty, historic meaning and triumph over great odds."

—*Georgia King and S. Evon Barvinchack*
Greencastle, Pennsylvania

We Held Our Breath Going Over The Cornish-Windsor

I WAS LUCKY to grow up near the Cornish-Windsor Bridge, which spans the Connecticut River between Cornish, New Hampshire and Windsor, Vermont.

My parents used that bridge to try and keep us noisy kids quiet. Whenever we rode through it, we were required to keep very still and hold our breath in reverence. That was difficult, since at 460 feet, the Cornish-Windsor is the longest covered bridge in the United States!

I later walked across this bridge my first 2 years of high school. It sheltered me from the harsh winter winds howling up and down the valley while I waited for the school bus.

My mother's aunt told me a story about when she was very young. She and her father had taken the horse and carriage from Windsor to Cornish. Her father instructed her to stay inside the carriage and not to let the reins get under the horse's tail while he went inside a local business.

The horse flicked its tail to swish a fly off his rump, and his tail landed right over the reins. The frightened horse took off at full gallop—tossing my great-aunt around in the carriage like a salad.

The toll keeper at the bridge saw what was happening and dropped the toll gate. But it landed squarely between the horse and the carriage. The horse broke free and was found at home in its stall.

Today, the Cornish-Windsor Covered Bridge is important as ever. It's the only connection to medical care, ambulance service, high school, gasoline, shopping and employment for my small New Hampshire hometown.

During one spring thaw, floodwaters and chunks of ice bigger than cars moved the bridge 13 inches off its piers. I was working with the local rescue squad during the flooding and was on the bridge when it was being bombarded by the ice. In fact, I was the last person to get off the bridge before it was closed.

The closure for repairs lasted over 2 years. It was an economic disaster for the area.

Covered bridges seemed the norm to me, growing up in the mountains of northern New England. In the city where I now live, the nearest I get to a covered bridge are the glass-enclosed walkways that cross over the streets.

In high school, 25 years ago, I painted a picture of the Cornish-Windsor Bridge. The picture hangs in my living room today, but looking at a picture of "my special bridge" just isn't the same. —*Stephen Tracy*
Louisville, Kentucky

So Much for That Theory!

WHENEVER I drive through the lovely Chiselville Covered Bridge at Sunderland, Vermont, I remember the time I tried to ride my mare across the bridge to take her to a horse farm 10 miles away for breeding.

As we approached the bridge, she took one look at the Roaring Branch River many feet below and absolutely would not step onto the bridge. So much for the theory that covered bridges look like barns to entice animals inside!

My husband came along and after trying unsuccessfully to pull her across, he wrapped his jacket around her head. We turned her around several times and then she walked through.

On the way back a number of days later, I had no trouble getting her to cross the bridge. She seemed to know it was the way home. —*Patricia Dupree*
Manchester Center, Vermont

"THEY SAY absence makes the heart grow fonder, and I really became attached to the Henry Covered Bridge in Mingo Creek Park after I moved away," writes James Rosh of Yardley, Pennsylvania. "When I'd return to western Pennsylvania, I'd always take my nieces to see the covered bridge—that's them sitting on the wall. Soon they fell in love with that bridge, too."

I Take Three Cameras When I Go 'Bridging'

By Rev. Paul Myers, Fostoria, Ohio

I started visiting covered bridges as a hobby in the early 1970's, when I was a pastor serving a parish in Maryland. There were four bridges near the town of Thurmont, and I'd seen each of them.

By the mid-'80's, I became more serious about visiting and photographing covered bridges. In fact, I now take three cameras—one for color prints, one for slides I use in making covered bridge presentations and a video camera for making motion pictures.

I love visiting bridge sites because they're so peaceful and quiet. These wonderful surroundings on a summer day just bring out the best in a person.

Someone might say, "You see one bridge, you've seen them all." But that isn't the case. Each one is unique.

As you travel to a bridge, you notice the approach and the abutments. Does the roof overhang the opening? Are there windows or just long vents along the side? What truss design was used? When was it built? Who was the builder?

There are so many questions to ask, but that's what makes bridging such an interesting hobby.

"THE DIXON BRANCH Covered Bridge now sits in a park in Lewis, Ohio," reports Paul. "It was built in 1887 and is 50 feet long."

"THE SHORTEST covered bridge in Ohio is the Church Hill Road Bridge," comments Paul. "It's just 22 feet long and is located in the town of Elkton. It was built in 1870 with King Post trusses."

"THIS BEAUTY in Washington County, Ohio is known as the Hills/Hildreth Covered Bridge," notes Paul. "It's 122 feet long and was built in 1878. It spans the Little Muskingum River."

"THE Geer Mill/Humpback Covered Bridge crosses Raccoon Creek in Vinton County, Ohio," says Paul. "It's 165 feet long and was built in 1874. Unfortunately, it's not in near as good condition as the famous Humpback Bridge in Virginia."

Our Community Spirit Burned Brightly After the Bridge Fire

By Mrs. Richard Wagaman, Sabillasville, Maryland

On a morning in June 1991, someone stole a truck, parked it inside the Loy's Station Covered Bridge near Thurmont, Maryland and set it on fire. Residents were heartbroken. But within 2 years after the bridge was destroyed, reconstruction began.

As a fund-raiser, the Frederick County Covered Bridge Preservation Society sold shingles for $1 each ...with the buyers recognized by having their names written on the undersides of the shingles they bought before the shingles were installed on the bridge roof.

In just 8 days, 2,300 shingles were sold.

On the Fourth of July holiday weekend, volunteers got together to write the names on the shingles and place them on the roof. They worked from 6 a.m. until dark in 95° heat. Members of the community flocked to the site with food and drinks for the volunteers.

Louise Loy, a 10th-generation descendant of the family for whom the bridge is named, traveled from Florida to cut the ribbon at the rededication in June 1994. This is how the bridge looks today (below).

"THE Langley Covered Bridge near Centreville is one of the bridges we found on our tour of Michigan," says Helen Oechsle. "It's 282 feet long and was built across Sturgis Lake in 1887."

I Enjoy Drives with Mom and Dad

By Helen Delnay Oechsle, Jackson, Michigan

Ever since the 1940's, our family has had a tradition of going for a drive. Back then, it was the one entertainment Mom and Dad could afford. We've continued to enjoy it through the decades.

Now, whenever Mom and Dad return to Michigan in summer from their retirement home in Florida, we start out with no particular destination in mind, travel the backroads to soak up the serenity and scenery and enjoy dinner in some small town before returning home.

We had an especially enjoyable time one summer looking for three of the remaining covered bridges in the state. The challenge of finding these bridges and spending time to inspect them and read about their history while enjoying the scenery made for 2 very special days with Mom and Dad.

The pictures I took—like this one of the Langley Covered Bridge in Centreville (above)—bring back fond memories of our time together exploring southern Michigan.

"MY FAMILY has lived just 3 miles from the Jackson Covered Bridge for over 100 years. I learned to swim under its shelter in Sugar Creek," recalls Janet Williams of Redkey, Indiana. "Proverbs 22:28 says, 'Remove not the ancient landmark which thy fathers have set.' How appropriate that proverb is to our covered bridges!"

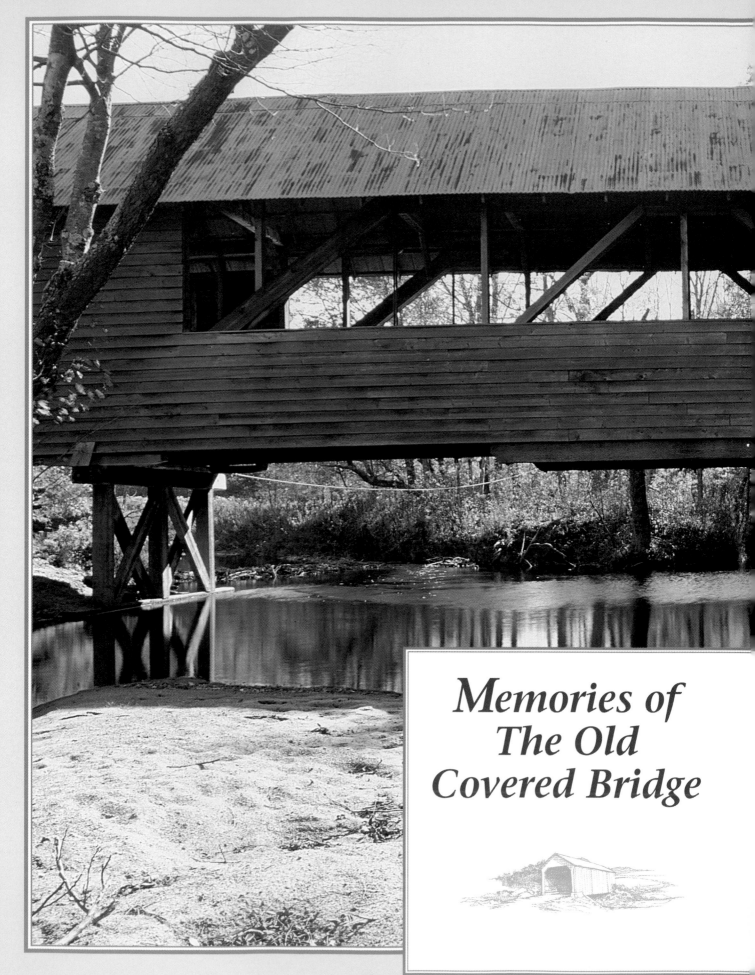

Memories of The Old Covered Bridge

Bump Covered Bridge, Campton, New Hampshire—Photo: Ray Packard

Though it's no longer used,
   It stands to remind us
Of times in the long, long ago,
   When neighbors had time to visit,
And life was easy and slow.

It could accommodate
   Only one lane of traffic,
But most folks were glad to wait
   For a neighbor to make his way
Through the bridge—
   Whatever his horse's gait.

Very often they stopped to chat awhile
   Or, sometimes just a nod of the head
Conveyed their message of friendliness—
   Without a word being said.

A traveler sometimes used
   Its welcome shelter
From a snowstorm or blinding rain,
   'Til the sun reappeared
And the sky became blue
   And he took up his journey again.

I'm quite sure we'd be well entertained
   If our covered bridges could talk;
It was said lovers often tarried there
   When out for an evening walk.

How sad it would be if we didn't preserve
   This symbol of long, long ago,
When neighbors had time to visit,
   And life was easy and slow.
      —Georgia Berkey, Osterburg, Pennsylvania

Grandma Crossed the Bean Blossom on Her Sales Route

By P.L. Phillips, Payson, Arizona

During the 1920's, my mother and grandparents lived near the Bean Blossom Covered Bridge (pictured at right), located just south of the crossroads town of Bean Blossom, Indiana.

My grandmother was a traveling saleslady. She drove a horse and buggy across this bridge on her travels to and from Nashville, Indiana to sell Pitkins Products.

My mother often tells of a flood year when my grandfather drove a stake in the front yard, indicating the high-water point at which he would have to evacuate the family. Fortunately, the water never reached that mark.

"THE PACKSADDLE Covered Bridge in Somerset County, Pennsylvania is among my collection of 600 covered bridge photos," shares Pat Kraeuter.

I Cherish Searching for Bridges With My Husband

By Pat Kraeuter, West Mifflin, Pennsylvania

I started taking pictures of covered bridges over 10 years ago on camping trips with my husband. It seemed like every time we camped, it rained. No matter—the covered bridge we were camping near would keep us dry.

You can explore a time forgotten in some of the remote bridges that are still covered with old advertisements. You can relax under their spans and marvel at the expert craftsmanship of the carpenters who built them.

If you're lucky and it's a sunny spring day, you can fish in the reflection of the bridge and listen to the birth of a new season in the songs of the birds.

I now have over 600 photos of covered bridges from Pennsylvania, Ohio, Maryland and Michigan (see one above). Many are taken on rainy days, but their memories keep me warm and dry.

I don't have one special bridge, because each holds a different story. But I do miss the bridges that have been washed away...that lay along the creek bed for years until funding is obtained for their repairs. I'm thankful that I have photographs of many of these bridges while they were still standing.

I cherish the great circle of friends who support me in finding more bridges to photograph. But most of all, I enjoy the adventure with my husband—finding the next covered bridge tucked away in some peaceful valley where life and time move at a much slower pace.

THE MAGNIFICENT Albany Covered Bridge crosses the Swift River at Conway, New Hampshire. It's 120 feet long and was built in 1858. Thanks to Barbara and Charles Lindberg of Lynnwood, Washington for sharing this photo.

God Led Us to the Albany Bridge

By Maurine Carter, Ventura, California

I received a beautiful picture postcard from a friend in August of 1990.

On one side was a message wishing me well on my upcoming surgery. On the other side was a picture of a covered bridge over a stream and a Scriptural inset that read, "Ask and it shall be given you; seek and ye shall find; knock and it will be opened unto you. Matthew 7:7."

The bridge wasn't identified on the postcard and there was no clue of its location. To me, it was just another covered bridge. But the message and the Scripture verse touched me. So I set the card aside from all my other cards of encouragement.

Two years later, my husband, O.J., and I traveled to Boston for a visit with our nephew and his wife. They'd prearranged for us to accompany them to New Hampshire. There we'd stay in a cabin to experience the beauty of autumn in New England and to celebrate O.J.'s 78th birthday.

On O.J.'s birthday, we packed a picnic, including a birthday cake, and set out to find a special place for the celebration. We crisscrossed the Swift River, seeing at least three covered bridges along the way.

We decided to go farther to a more pristine area. When we reached the Albany Covered Bridge, O.J. and I got out of the car and walked across it.

We had our picture taken peeking out between the cross beams. The river was wide and shallow. So we were able to walk out onto huge boulders in the riverbed. There we spread out our lunch, gave thanks and celebrated the occasion.

We returned home to California with packets of beautiful photos of autumn foliage in New England, family and several covered bridges. I put the photos in a special file box and kept them on the coffee table for easy viewing.

But the story doesn't end just yet. The following spring I was rearranging closets as part of my spring housecleaning. There, stuck between some old boxes, I discovered the postcard my friend had sent me years before. And there it was—our covered bridge, the very one in New Hampshire where we picnicked and had our picture taken! The stream was there—even the rocks where we'd sat and had our birthday celebration!

Call it coincidence if you wish. But we feel God led us to that particular bridge for a very special celebration...where He gave us a deeper appreciation for His beautiful creation and for His care and protection during my illness.

I Saw My First Covered Bridge Thanks to Shirley Temple

By Ruby Ward, La Habra, California

I became fascinated with covered bridges about 6 years ago, while on my way to a Shirley Temple Collectors Convention in Newark, New Jersey.

This trek gave me the opportunity to make a side trip to Connecticut and visit a friend. I'd never seen a covered bridge before, so my friend and her sister took me to the Silk Road Covered Bridge at Bennington, Vermont (above). Later, we visited the Old Sturbridge Village in Sturbridge, Massachusetts, where I saw my second covered bridge. I was hooked!

I've since seen covered bridges in Oregon and Missouri while traveling to more collectors conventions. Thanks, Shirley, for your role in introducing me to covered bridges.

Here's an Idea for Sprucing Up Your Bridge

I am trying to put together a program similar to the "Adopt a Highway" program for our covered bridges in Chester County, Pennsylvania. It's called "Adopt a Covered Bridge" and is designed to accomplish three goals:

1. Clean up the litter around covered bridges.
2. Spruce up the bridge areas with flowers and paint over graffiti.
3. Repair the structures and develop parking areas nearby.

I'm president of the Chester County Tourist Bureau, and our covered bridges are a unique attraction. We have 15 covered bridges, and 11 of them are still in use.

—*Karl Klingelhoeffer Jr.*
Berwyn, Pennsylvania

"WHEN MOST people think of New Jersey, they think of traffic, hustle and bustle and a lot of people—but there's one spot that reminds us of how life once was," note Nikki Waples and Glen Stupienski of Woodcliff Lake. "On the outskirts of Sergeantsville, the Green Sergeants Covered Bridge stretches its timbers 84 feet over Wickeheoke Creek. Built in 1866, it's the last covered highway bridge in the state."

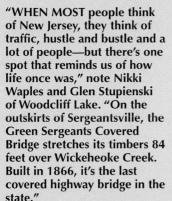

"SCIPIO COVERED BRIDGE, in Jennings County, Indiana, is one of our favorites," notes Anne Lanham of Morgantown, North Carolina. "My husband and I have taken pictures of it in all seasons, but our trip to photograph it in winter was the most memorable. While trying for the best vantage point to shoot the picture, I stepped into a deep hole and sank up to my waist in snow. My husband came to my rescue and pulled me out. It was worth it, however, because this picture turned out to be the best one we've taken of the bridge so far."

Our Bridge Builder Went Barefoot To Save His Shoes

By Wayne Marshfield, Hamden, New York

Our community is proud of Hamden Covered Bridge, which spans the west branch of the Delaware River (pictured at right). It's one of the few covered bridges remaining in Delaware County, New York and one of only 12 long-truss covered bridges left in the United States.

The bridge was built in 1859 by Robert Murray for $1,000. At the time, Murray lived 10 miles away in Andes. He walked to the bridge site each Monday morning, boarded out during the week and hiked home on Saturday night. Legend has it that the frugal Scotsman left his work shoes at the covered bridge so as not to wear them out.

Four windows were installed in the bridge in later years because kids were knocking out the hemlock side panels in order to fish from the bridge.

A metal roof was installed when a railroad track was laid 50 feet from the bridge. It was feared a burning ember from a locomotive would ignite the wooden roof.

During our devastating flood on January 19, 1996, a concrete county bridge a half mile upstream was heavily damaged and closed for several weeks. The covered bridge came through the flood un-

scathed and accepted the concrete bridge's traffic (up to its 3-ton load limit) while it was closed.

I've heard that covered bridges have roofs so cattle and horses would cross them, thinking they were entering a barn. I'm not so sure that's the reason after witnessing someone trying to lead a mule across the Hamden Covered Bridge. He ended up leading that mule through the river instead.

Our community hopes to preserve this beautiful bit of history for our children and their children. It will be restored in 1999 at a cost of approximately $700,000.

Enslow Covered Bridge Bears Our Family Name...Sort of

By James Endslow, Mt. Joy, Pennsylvania

We have lots of fascinating bridges in Pennsylvania. But the one I'm most enamored with is the Enslow Covered Bridge in Perry County (pictured at right). That's because it bears my name—sort of.

The Enslow Covered Bridge was built by my great-great-grandfather, Samuel S. Enslow. Samuel lived just several hundred yards from where the bridge crosses Sherman's Creek. He operated a gristmill and a blacksmith shop on the banks of the creek. The mill and the smithy are long gone, but the sturdy brick farmhouse he built in 1864 still stands and is occupied.

The bridge was built in 1904 at a cost of $2,250. It was damaged in a flood in September 1996, the result of 10 inches of rain from Hurricane Fran. But it has since been repaired.

The difference in spelling of the Enslow and Endslow names is the result of a family feud between

Samuel's son William (my great-grandfather) and his brother over a horse trade. Samuel was so angered that he changed his name!

"FOR ME, covered bridges represent survival. The old structures have survived from a time long gone. And their craft work, unique to its time in history, lives on as well," writes Ruth James of Napa, California. "I've found them in some of the most scenic out-of-the-way locations, which always makes a covered bridge a pleasure to visit. Here's one of my favorites—the Knights Ferry Covered Bridge at Knights Ferry, California."

A Trip to The Covered Bridge

What makes it so inviting?
Come and share my dream.
It's the road I've never traveled,
The bridge I haven't seen;

It's the countryside inviting,
The path I've never trod,
It's the majesty of beauty;
It's the handiwork of God.

It's the architecture; it's the trusses;
It's man's skills upon display;
It's the history of a bygone era,
Less hurried than today.

It's the mill, the falls, the stream itself,
The uncertainty of what is just ahead.
It's the challenge of the search,
And the discovery of where it has led.

It's the style, design or use,
Each unique in its own way;
The bridge is like a memory link
Binding today with yesterday.

I think of others using it
As shelter from the storm,
Or a pleasant trip to church
On a bright and sunny morn.

What makes it so inviting?
I guess I like to roam.
But as the evening shadows lengthen,
I have to head toward home.

Hopefully someday
Another trip I'll chart,
But for today my wanderlust
Has fulfilled the dream
Within my heart.

—*Kay Starkey, Homeworth, Ohio*

Bridgers Sure Are Friendly Folks

FOR ABOUT 25 YEARS, my husband and I have traveled across the country visiting covered bridges. We've seen 361 to date.

As you might suspect, there aren't many covered bridge enthusiasts in Texas, where we live. But that doesn't stop us from seeking out people with whom we can share our hobby.

A friend sent me an article on covered bridges from *The Washington Post*. The story quoted bridging enthusiast Myron Miller of Hershey, Pennsylvania, who owned thousands of slides of covered bridges. I remarked to my husband that I wanted to meet this man. So I looked up his address at the library and wrote him.

I could hardly believe it, but a few months later, we were overnight guests in Myron's home and looking at his collection of slides.

Myron was treasurer of the Theodore Burr Covered Bridge Society of Pennsylvania, and our visit coincided with their monthly meeting. So we were invited to attend the meeting, too.

I corresponded with Myron for several years before his death at age 72. He taught me that opportunities abound, if we only take the time to look and act.
—*Joanne Druce, Cibolo, Texas*

Mom Paints Pictures of the Old Bridge for Charity

THE WASHINGTON MILL Covered Bridge was destroyed by vandals in 1968. To keep the memory of this bridge alive in our community, my mother,

"MY FATHER-IN-LAW, Harold Price, lives on the same farm where he was born and raised," notes Sonja Price of Lewisburg, Ohio. "The farm is located on Lewisburg-Western Road, only a half mile from the Geeting Covered Bridge. The bridge was built across Price Creek in 1894. Harold's mother, Elsie, carried water to the 30 men constructing the bridge when she was 7 years old. When they laid the first plank across the floor beams, she was the first person they let walk across the bridge."

Mary Clark, decided in 1973 to paint a picture of the bridge and donate it to the Bellbrook Lions Club to be raffled off at their annual carnival. She has continued to do this every year since.

A few years ago, Mother had a stroke and was very ill. But she was still determined to finish her painting for the Lions Club. She is 78 now and still painting the bridge to keep its memory alive.
—*Pat Trimble, Bellbrook, Ohio*

"THE LEOTA Covered Bridge over Cooney Creek is Scott County, Indiana's newest covered bridge," says Helen Goben of Scottsburg, Indiana. "It was dedicated in August 1995 at the intersection of two of the state's oldest roads— Bloomington Trail, which was originally a buffalo trail to the salt licks in Kentucky, and Leota Road, which was surveyed by a Revolutionary War soldier. That's me and my daughter, Betty Robbins, all decked out for the bridge's dedication."

"IN 1920, my grandparents and their nine children moved to a farm adjacent to Kidds Mill Covered Bridge in Mercer County, Pennsylvania," notes Shirley Kather of Hadley. "My mother and her brothers and sisters walked across that bridge daily to go to school. During summers, they enjoyed swimming and picnicking beside the bridge. The farm is now owned by the third generation of our family. The farm and the covered bridge bring back lots of happy memories for us."

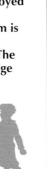

Clever Women Nixed the Nickel Toll

LEGEND has it that in the 1860's, two ladies in a buggy pulled by a mare approached the Bell's Ford Covered Toll Bridge in Jackson County, Indiana. When they inquired about the toll, the toll master said it was 5¢ for a man and a horse.

The ladies said that since neither of them was a man and the animal they were driving was a mare, the toll didn't apply to them. Then they crossed the bridge without paying! —*Fleeta Arthur*
Brownstown, Indiana

Great-Grandpa Was the Bridge Lamplighter

I FOUND an entry from 1885 in a book by the Zumbro Valley Historical Society in Goodhue County, Minnesota:

"According to the minutes of the City Council, $15.00 was paid to J. Andrews for lighting the lamp in the covered bridge."

John Andrews was my great-grandfather, and the sum was his payment for this nightly service for a year! —*Dorothy Swanson, Worthington, Minnesota*

We Lived by Arthur Godfrey's Bridge

FOR 16 YEARS, we lived next to the Cresson Bridge in Swanzey, New Hampshire. In 1953, this bridge was used by the famous entertainer Arthur Godfrey as a tie-in with a Chesterfield cigarette Christmas carton. The governor at the time, Hugh Gregg, flew to New York to present Arthur Godfrey with an honorary deed to the bridge. After that, folks in Swanzey referred to it as the Arthur Godfrey Bridge.

Living in the shadow of the bridge, we had lots of company. We often had buses drive into our yard and people running around taking pictures. Amazingly, most of my flowers and bushes remained intact.

Once a man slid sideways onto the bridge with his car. It took him over an hour to get out. Our doorbell rang many times from people needing to call a wrecker or a parent to come help. We met a lot of people and dried a few tears! It was worth all of the commotion, however, to live next to this famous bridge.
—*Mrs. Joseph Di Meco, Hampton, New Hampshire*

Twin Covered Bridges Were "Family Built"

MY ANCESTORS built the Twin Covered Bridges crossing Huntington Creek at Forks, Pennsylvania. The bridges, known as the East Paden and the West Paden, were built in 1850 and are the only twin covered bridges remaining in the U.S. (see a photo of the bridges on page 24).

My great-great-great-grandparents' home was located about half a block from these bridges. My great-great-great-grandmother traded food and other items with the Indians around the time the bridges were built. —*Margaret Paden May*
Arlington, Virginia

Ada Bridge Reminds Us of Peaceful Times

By Anne Penning, Ada, Michigan

My husband and I love to take walks through the Ada Covered Bridge (pictured above). It's located just 4 miles from our home in Ada, Michigan.

In the evening when the bridge and village are lit up by lanterns, it reminds us of days past when life's pace was slower and there was time for neighbors.

This bridge has been threatened many times over the years by floodwaters. It's said that farmers used to drive wagons loaded with stone onto the bridge during floods to hold it to the foundation.

"THIS COVERED BRIDGE spanning the South Umpqua River is the only access to Milo Adventist Academy, a boarding school operated by the Seventh-Day Adventist Church," notes Jenienne Kriegelstein of Days Creek, Oregon. "The bridge wasn't covered when it was built in 1962 to replace an old wooden bridge. However, area residents felt they'd lost part of their heritage. So the bridge was modified to make it a covered bridge. Alumni remember night swims at the bridge, and students still love to swing on the rope over the water on hot summer days."

You Can See Cattle Grazing From the Bridge

By Zelda Rowley, Mt. Rainier, Maryland

My favorite covered bridge is located at Strasburg, Pennsylvania in the heart of beautiful Pennsylvania Dutch country. It's a tiny bridge that spans Little Beaver Creek on the grounds of the Beaver Creek Farm Cabins in Lancaster County.

My favorite photo of the bridge is one I took from inside it, looking out the side window (below). That view is especially beautiful just after sunrise. Some mornings as you gaze downstream, you can catch a glimpse of sheep, goats and cattle in the field.

The Helmick Bridge Is Our 'Neighbor'

By Paulene Croft, Killbuck, Ohio

Our farm near Killbuck, Ohio has been in the family for four generations, and we're proud to have the Helmick Covered Bridge (pictured above) as our "neighbor".

It's located a mile from the farm and was built in 1863 while my two grandfathers, Henry Myers and Jonas Mullet, were away serving in the Civil War.

At the time, Helmick was a flourishing trade center. It had two mills, a post office, a school and a general store. The Helmick Bridge was integral for farmers to travel to and from the gristmills, one of which was operated by my great-uncle Stephen Mullet. I traveled through the bridge every day as a child on our school bus. I spent many hours playing there, too.

The Helmick Covered Bridge was closed to traffic in 1981. But with lots of planning, fund-raising and work, a committee of concerned citizens proudly restored the bridge 10 years later.

"OVER 50 years ago, my relatives gathered for family reunions under the big shade trees by Mary's Covered Bridge in Randolph County, Illinois," writes Myron Chunn of Steeleville. "This bridge crosses the Little Mary's River and was built as part of a plank toll road between the towns of Chester and Bremen. A two-horse wagon was charged a toll of 20¢. A man on horseback was charged 5¢ and a farmer with a hog or sheep was charged 2¢—unless he was driving a large number of animals. Then the toll was lowered to a penny per head."

Marsha Williamson Mohr

Visitors Are Welcome, But I Treasure Quiet Times

By Jill Beeler, Rosedale, Indiana

I live about three blocks from the Bridgeton Covered Bridge at Bridgeton, Indiana (pictured above). It was built in 1868—the same year my house was built.

When I was young, we'd ride horses through the covered bridge and the stream during summer. Sometimes, after a long day of detasseling corn, we'd cool off by tying a rope from the bridge and swinging into the water below. We could also count on good fishing under the bridge because the fish would hide in the bridge's shadow.

There are 32 covered bridges in our beautiful Parke County. So when I was older and could drive, my friends and I would sometimes go "bridge hopping" throughout the county and scare the couples who'd parked there.

Bridge hopping was especially popular at Halloween. You never knew who—or what—was hiding in the darkness of the bridges. Sometimes even a scarecrow would drop from the rafters!

I have young children of my own now, and I tell them about the fun I had at the bridges—well, most of it. My husband tells how he was baptized in the water under one of the bridges. Our family often bicycles to the nearby bridges, where we'll walk and talk quietly.

Sometimes I walk by myself to one of the bridges to listen and pray. It is a special sound and feeling. The windows in a covered bridge are like the picture frame to God's creation.

Grandma used to tell me about the days when she sat in the window of the Bridgeton Bridge and took in the quiet stream below. I've sat in the same window and tried to feel what it was like to be part of the past...and imagine the conversations held there over the years.

There are only about 125 people in my little hometown of Bridgeton. We don't have a grocery store or a gas station. But once a year there's a countywide Covered Bridge Festival that starts the second weekend of October and lasts 10 days. We estimate over 1 million people come from all over the world to attend.

The festival is exciting, and visitors are always welcome. But I also treasure the quiet times when I can walk through the bridge alone and talk to God once again.

"OUR FAMILY has enjoyed picnicking and camping at Allegheny State Park in western New York, especially since a wonderful bike path was developed around Red House Lake," relates Betsy Garfield of Frewsburg. "A beautiful covered bridge was built over a babbling brook along the bike path. Although it's not an old bridge, it already holds many memories for us. In fact, last Thanksgiving when our family met at the park for an old-fashioned dinner, there was no question where the family picture would be taken."

My Great-Grandpa's Bridge Still Stands Strong

ALLAMAN COVERED BRIDGE is special to me because it was built by my great-grandfather. It's one of the few covered bridges remaining in the state of Illinois.

Jacob Allaman, a barn and bridge builder in Pennsylvania, moved his family to Illinois in 1858. He built a number of barns and bridges in Henderson County. Two barns remain, but the Allaman Covered Bridge is the only bridge left.

According to Jacob's ledger, which we still have, the bridge was built in August and September of 1866 over Henderson Creek. The beams were cut to shape at a local lumberyard, then hauled to the bridge site, where Jacob and his crew of five men assembled them and finished the bridge. The carpenters were paid $1 per day for their work. The total cost of the bridge was $2,125.

The bridge carried traffic until 1934, when a new highway bridge was constructed. In 1935, the State of Illinois acquired the bridge. It was placed on the National Register of Historic Places in 1975.

A flood pushed the bridge from its abutments in July 1982 and floated it downstream, where ironically it lodged against the new highway bridge. Thankfully, a group of Historical Society members, with help from the Department of Transportation, decided to salvage the bridge.

We disassembled the bridge and made a list of new timbers that would be needed. These were ordered from a mill in Wyoming, delivered to a local sawmill, where rough cuts were made, then shipped to Pine Bluff, Arkansas for pressure treatment with a fire retardant. When the lumber arrived back from Arkansas, a local carpenter and his crew made all the final cuts in the beams and other parts of the bridge using the original templates.

During July, August and September of 1984, we put the bridge together, using 75% of the original beams. We then rolled it across the creek on big steel beams to its original location.

Thanks to the efforts of many people to preserve a piece of local history, this bridge was dedicated to future generations in a ceremony on September 29, 1984.

—*John Allaman, Kirkwood, Illinois*

The Gilkey Bridge Is a Great Place to "Cat Fish"

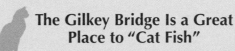

MY HUSBAND and I decided to do some fishing and rafting on Thomas Creek on a warm July day. So we loaded the car and headed to the Gilkey Covered Bridge near Scio, Oregon—the drop-off point for the car where we would land after our long raft journey.

As we were leaving the car, I heard a noise coming from underneath the bridge. We worked our way over rocks and through mud puddles toward the noise in a deep hole around one of the bridge supports.

Inside the hole was a little ball of fluff—a kitten that started purring the instant I pulled it from the hole.

We brought the kitten back to our car and gave it some food and water while we figured out what to do with it. We saw no signs of a mother cat. But we decided to leave it—just in case it belonged to someone nearby. We reasoned that if the kitten was still there when we returned from our raft trip, we'd take it home with us.

But when we set the kitten down, our hearts broke. It could barely move. Its front legs were hurt and it hobbled after us, mewing at the top of its lungs.

Of course, we took it with us. The cat is now very healthy and follows us everywhere we go. We like to think of Gilkey Bridge as a great place to "cat fish"! —*Celeste Starr, Salem, Oregon*

Dad Never Smoked Again!

MY FATHER, Charles Marsh, was born in 1881. He attended a one-room school in Cambridge, New York. During the noon hour, he'd walk through the covered bridge over the Battenkill River to get the family mail.

One day as he performed his daily errand, Dad acquired a cigar and smoked it as he crossed the bridge. He became so sick that he couldn't attend classes that afternoon. But the good news was he *never* smoked again! —*Dorothy Marsh Macauley Cambridge, New York*

"I'VE LOCATED and photographed 205 covered bridges in 18 states, including this one of the Fisher Railroad Bridge at Wolcott, Vermont," says Paul Parrott of Lexington, Kentucky. "My goal is to eventually see and photograph at least 300 of these priceless treasures. The hunt is half the fun. It's an exhilarating moment when, after wondering just how lost you are, you suddenly see that grand old bridge standing there. You say, 'Aha! There you are!' And it seems to say, 'I've been waiting for you!' "

"MY HUSBAND and I are thankful we were able to locate and photograph all 219 registered, and three unregistered, covered bridges in Pennsylvania. This photo of the Dellville Bridge in Perry County is one of them," relates Dorothy Keller of Myerstown. "We worked on the project from July 1996 to August 1997. Although we were in our mid-70's, we crisscrossed the state, driving over the mountains and on remote roads. It was a challenge at times, but the folks we met along the way were so friendly and helpful. It was worth every difficulty to locate and enjoy these important parts of our state's history."

A Construction Crane Dropped Our Bridge into the River

By Charles Clevenger, New Boston, Ohio

I grew up in rural Scioto County, Ohio in the mid-1930's and lived about a mile from the Tuttleville Covered Bridge (pictured above). As an enterprising lad, I rode my much-traveled fenderless bicycle through the bridge every Saturday to deliver my small bundle of *Grit* newspapers (at 5¢ per copy) to a few far-flung customers.

There was a shaded deep pool of cold water—locally known as the "icebox"—downstream just a couple hundred yards from the bridge. It served as a popular swimmin' hole for us kids.

Construction on the bridge began just before the Civil War. But the project was suspended during the war years, and the bridge was finally completed in 1867. Local folklore says the general contractor was a young man only 19 years of age when the bridge was completed.

In 1983, the bridge was scheduled to be torn down and replaced with a modern bridge. A preservation committee raised money to have the Tut-tleville Bridge dismantled and reassembled at a suitable location to stand as a monument of its place in history.

Two huge cranes were positioned—one on each side of the river. While secured to the cranes, the bridge was cut into halves. Then each crane was to lift its half from the bridge abutments and swing it to the riverbank, where it could be systematically disassembled.

But tragedy befell the project. One of the cranes tipped over with its heavy load, sending the once-proud bridge crashing into the water! The salvage crew fished the pieces from the river and hauled them to a nearby farm. But many of those great beams and trusses were broken beyond repair and couldn't be reassembled.

The pieces remain stacked and in an open field, where they are covered with heavy tarpaulins for protection from the weather. I hope resurrection day will still come.

"MY WIFE and I have photographed about 300 covered bridges in 22 states," shares Francis Geist of Mishawaka, Indiana. "One of our favorite photos is this one of the Wolf Bridge in Knox County, Illinois. I was hanging from a branch over the river with one hand to get the shot. I didn't even notice the swimmer cooling off under the bridge until I got my film back. Unfortunately, the bridge is gone now—burned by vandals."

I've Shed Many Tears for My Bridge

By Karen Uhlenbrock, Cincinnati, Ohio

Eagle Creek Covered Bridge was located in south-western Ohio—3 miles south of Decatur, my home-town.

When my son, now 28, was barely a year old, his grandfather took him across the bridge for the first time. After going through and coming out the other side, my son turned around with eyes as wide as saucers. He had a big grin on his face as if to say, "What happened?" My mother and I still laugh about it.

Eagle Creek Covered Bridge was brutal-ly washed away in a March 1997 flood. The water came with such force that it totally destroyed the old bridge and damaged a new bridge built next to it. In just a mat-ter of minutes, it was reduced to a pile of rubble.

I've shed a lot of tears for my bridge. It's just a memory now, but it'll always hold a special place in my heart. The floodwa-ters can't wash that away from me.

We Toured Every Covered Bridge In the State

By Elaine Cooley, Louisville, Kentucky

"WE FOUND the Johnson Creek Covered Bridge in Robertson County, Kentucky," says Elaine. "It's 112 feet long and was built in 1874."

After our retirement a few years ago, my husband and I decided to visit all the covered bridges in Kentucky.

What fun we have had! Covered bridges aren't located on interstate highways—they're tucked away in remote sections of the country that offer picturesque beauty.

After making our first two bridge visits, we moved our trips to later in the fall, when more of the leaves had fallen from the trees. That way, we could get the full view of the bridges.

At one time there were 400 covered bridges in the state. But there were 13 at the time we started searching...and one of them, the Switzer Bridge in Franklin County, was destroyed in the spring flood of 1997. I'm grateful we were able to see this special bridge before it was lost.

"THE Beech Fork/Mooresville Covered Bridge (left) is located in Washington County, Kentucky," notes Elaine. "It was built in 1865 and is now closed to traffic. It's 211 feet long."

"THIS WEATHERED old bridge (below) is the Dover Covered Bridge in Mason County, Kentucky," explains Elaine. "It's 63 feet long and was built over Lee's Creek in 1835."

"THE BABY of the bunch is the Valley/Pike Covered Bridge, also in Mason County," Elaine shares. "It's only 35 feet long and was built in 1925."

"WHEN I STOOD on the Delta Bridge in Keokuk County, Iowa, it spanned the years and transported me to a time when life was gentle and travel was slow-paced, without horns, sirens and 'road rage'," notes Joan Gilliam of Del Valle, Texas, who snapped this photo. "America's automotive progress has been exciting, but we lost something in the process—serenity."

Grandpa Donated Lumber To Repair the Delta Bridge

By Penny Gillett Silvius, Fresno, California

The covered bridge in Delta, Iowa (pictured above) has been near and dear to my family for at least five generations.

My grandfather, Homer Rohloff, often reminisced about having to haul snow into the wooden structure so his horse-drawn sleigh could pass through.

My mother says she took the bridge for granted when she was growing up. But she does recall making a special trip there during her childhood with a girlfriend to add their initials to the other carvings in the bridge.

As a child, I felt such excitement when our trips to Grandma and Grandpa's house led us through the old covered bridge.

My sister, Bonnie, and I loved to walk on the bridge and read the carved names proclaiming the love of couples that had crossed the bridge before us.

Bonnie's name was carved in large letters in one rafter way at the top of the bridge. I remember wondering who might have a crush on my sister to go to so much trouble.

In the 1950's, the siding on the bridge was deteriorating, and the county didn't have the money to repair it. Since the bridge was so special to my grandfather, he furnished the siding by giving the county a barn he wasn't using. Grandpa's siding is still on that bridge today.

In later years, my grandparents also donated land next to the bridge to be used as a park. I've always been proud of the sign that bears their names as the donors. That's them standing by the sign in the photo (inset above).

The Delta Bridge was closed to vehicle traffic in the 1970's. It had served well as a crossing for over 100 years.

But it still carries people as they walk into the past...and some new support beams offer carving places for another generation of sweethearts to permanently declare their devotion to one another!

Chapter Five

HAUNTED
Memories

The huge timbers of covered bridges creak and groan, fog rises from the waters below...and the bridges' dark shadows are perfect hiding places for critters and pranksters. No wonder ghost stories abound.

I Had This Feeling We Weren't Alone

By Kimberly Kuncl, Omaha, Nebraska

Huge evergreens towered over us as we walked along the road, which was banked by tall grass and weeds. There was an eerie silence.

As we looked up at the trees, it was as though they were staring at us. Wind whispered through them, as if telling them that strangers had invaded their territory.

Ominous Looking

We rounded a curve, and there, at the bottom of a hill, was the Creamery Bridge. It looked ominous surrounded by overgrown trees and brush. We could now hear the sound of rushing water from a nearby waterfall on West Hill Brook.

There was just something about this bridge that said no one was welcome. But we'd come a long way and wanted to explore. The only signs of recent human activity were campfire remains.

My husband, Eric, and I honeymooned in Vermont after our June 1997 wedding. I'm a native Nebraskan, so it had always been my dream to see New England, including its covered bridges.

We stayed at a bed-and-breakfast in northern Vermont, from which we struck out each day to do our covered bridge sight-seeing. We soon discovered if you aren't familiar with the territory, covered bridges aren't always easy to find. But that made it fun.

I was intrigued with one particular bridge I'd read about in our guidebook—the Creamery Bridge (pictured above) near Montgomery. It was abandoned… and supposedly haunted.

Once Eric saw the phrase "tricky to find" in our book, he was immediately soured by the idea of seeking it out. But I was eager to search for a forgotten bridge—and maybe some lost spirits. After a short newlywed debate, we were on our way.

Our book cautioned that the abandoned dirt road where the bridge stood wasn't in great condition. (In Nebraska, we call these minimum maintenance roads!) Our rented economy car turned out to be no match for this road, which looked more like a hiking trail. We parked, got out and walked.

The bridge itself wasn't the prettiest we'd seen. It certainly showed its age (built in 1883), with holes in the floor and an extremely weathered appearance. It looked as if Mother Nature was taking back the timbers that had once belonged to her.

As we sat and stared at the remains of this little bridge, it was fun to imagine what this span had been like in its prime. Who'd traveled across it? I'm sure teams of horses and wagons had crossed that bridge time and again, and young boys had used it on their way to their favorite fishing spots.

A Haunting Presence

As we sat there, I began to feel as if someone else was with us…maybe the spirit of someone from long ago who also was fond of this bridge.

Perhaps my imagination was getting a little too carried away, but I don't think Eric and I were alone that day. If there was a haunting presence, I don't think "it" wanted to frighten us. Maybe it just wanted to let us know we were welcome to look but not to stay.

Or, maybe it was just being nice because it knew we were a couple of crazy honeymooners from a faraway place called Nebraska.

Yankee Jim Was Hanged for A Crime He Didn't Commit

By Louise Kiel, Houston, Texas

It's no wonder the Bridgeport Covered Bridge in Nevada County, California is haunted.

Back in the 1850's, folks hanged a fellow by the name of Yankee Jim from the bridge for rustling cattle. People came from miles around to watch the hanging. Then, after it was too late, they discovered he didn't commit the crime.

But Jim was a man of ill-repute. Townspeople felt no remorse and decided he was better off hanged!

Present-day residents have a little more compassion for Yankee Jim. They put on a Halloween-inspired presentation called "Ghosts of Bridgeport" in which they portray various historical Bridgeport characters, including David Wood, the man who built the 233-foot bridge across the South Fork of the Yuba River back in 1862. Yankee Jim is still "hanged", but at least he's been given a proper burial!

The Bridgeport Bridge is the longest single-span covered bridge in the West. It now stands as a memorial to the miners and pioneers of 19th-century California.

In those days, it was part of the Virginia Turnpike Company toll road, which served northern-California gold mines and the Nevada Comstock lode. At its peak, 100 freight wagons crossed the bridge each day. The toll for an eight-horse team and wagon was $6. A person could walk across the bridge for 25¢.

LONGEST SPAN IN THE WEST. Thanks to Ruth James of Napa, California for sharing the photo above of Bridgeport Covered Bridge. The venerable structure was built in 1862.

"AREN'T ALL covered bridges haunted when the sky is dark, the moon is barely shining, the boards are wet on a foggy night and the bridge is the only place to find shelter?" asks Tony Siegmann of Middletown, Ohio. "Personally, I wouldn't be caught in a covered bridge under those conditions...although I did photograph the Bean Blossom Bridge outside Nashville, Indiana at night by the light of my high-beam headlights."

We Spooked the Halloween Spooks

I STILL CHUCKLE about the Halloween when my sister-in-law and I decided we needed to spook the spooks who were hiding in the rafters of the Bartonsville Covered Bridge at Rockingham, Vermont.

There were some teenagers from the village hiding in the rafters of the bridge, doing their best to scare the young children who were trick-or-treating. They were dropping rotten apples, eggs and water balloons on whoever crossed the bridge.

We loaded our pockets with apples that had fallen to the ground in my front yard and sneaked down to the bridge. We tossed those soft rotten apples, and they made a wonderful thud as they struck the tin roof of the bridge.

It quickly became safe for the little trick-or-treaters to cross, as those teens came pouring out of the bridge to see what was attacking. It was such fun!

I also have fond memories of when the bridge was closed for restoration and repair. Villagers had to make a 3-mile detour on a dirt road, which passed through a barnyard that was notoriously difficult during the spring mud season.

Everyone hoped the bridge would be reopened prior to mud season, but it wasn't finished until June. Although we were eager to begin using the bridge again, we kept the detour signs up one more night...for a celebration. We set up long tables near the bridge and some inside it for refreshments. We ran an extension cord to the bridge so we could have music for dancing in the bridge that evening.

It was a grand reopening party!   —*Nancy Adams*
White River Junction, Vermont

Uncle John Couldn't Outrun This Ghost

MY DAD lived near Paint Creek in Ross County, Ohio when he was growing up. He's 92 years old now and still loves to tell about the two covered bridges that spanned the creek.

Shott's Bridge had a reputation among the local citizens for being haunted. Dad's Uncle John lived in the area and was on his way home late one night. It was dark, of course—and even darker in that bridge. But Uncle John needed to walk through it to get home.

Uncle John had heard all the ghost stories—and believed them. So he took off his shoes before starting through the bridge. He could run faster with his shoes off and figured he could outrun even a ghost.

About halfway through the bridge, he ran smack into something big. But it wasn't a ghost—it was a

cow that had come in from the wind. I wonder who was scared the most!
—*Chloe Webb*
Fort Myers Beach, Florida

Stranger in Town Outsmarted the Ghosts

MY FATHER told me a story about a family from Kentucky who settled near the little town of Lewis Creek, Indiana long before my time.

Their house was near the Lewis Creek Covered Bridge on the outskirts of town. The wife used to cross the bridge whenever she went to the store.

One day three boys decided to play a trick on her. Each one sneaked a white sheet from his house. Then they climbed up the arch beams of the bridge and hung the sheets from the rafters...hoping the lady would think they were ghosts. They hid nearby—waiting and watching in eager anticipation.

Finally, the lady came out of the store carrying a bag of groceries. As she entered the bridge, she looked up and saw the dangling sheets. But instead of screaming and running away as the boys had hoped, she set down her bag, climbed up the arch beams and took down the sheets. After neatly folding them across her arm, she picked up her bag and went home.

The boys looked at each other in dismay. What were they going to do? In those days, sheets were valuable commodities, and soon one of the mothers noticed she was missing a sheet. Then the second mother and the third mother discovered that they, too, were missing sheets.

It seemed like more than just a coincidence that all three mothers were missing sheets at the same time. So, reluctantly, one of the boys 'fessed up about the ghosts in Lewis Creek Covered Bridge.
—*Carol Cochran, Kykotsmovi Village, Arizona*

You Can Still Hear Cries From the Roseman Covered Bridge

THE Roseman Covered Bridge is associated with romance ever since its starring role in the movie *Bridges of Madison County*. So it's ironic that the bridge also has a reputation for being haunted.

Legend has it that on a dark night in 1893, two posses were formed to hunt down an escapee from the Madison County jail. As they approached the Roseman Covered Bridge from opposite banks of the Middle River, they saw the man enter the bridge. Both posses spurred their horses to the bridge to prevent the criminal from fleeing. The trapped escapee uttered a wild cry—then somehow vanished through the roof of the bridge.

Folks said he must have been innocent to have been able to vanish into thin air. To this day, fisherman say they hear his cries from this haunted bridge.
—*Mrs. John Grandfield, Winterset, Iowa*

"THE Red Covered Bridge at Princeton, Illinois is supposed to be haunted," says Verla Huffaker of Malden. **"It seems that an old peddler used to camp there at night. One morning his horse and buggy were found there, but he'd disappeared and was never seen again."**
Thanks to Carol Moore of Clearwater, Florida for providing this photo.

Beware of the Edna Collins Bridge At Midnight

By Karla Perkins, Greencastle, Indiana

One drawback to covered bridges was that thieves and animals could hide in the dark corners, and unsuspecting travelers couldn't see them.

Imagine entering a bridge and having a prankster jump out at you...or stumbling upon a family of skunks or cows napping in the middle of the bridge. So naturally there were rumors of bridges being haunted.

The Edna Collins Bridge (at left) is the baby of all covered bridges in Indiana. It's only 80 feet long.

Many years ago, a young woman and her baby drowned in Little Walnut Creek, which flows below this bridge. Legend has it that if you drive your car into the bridge at midnight, the young woman will appear at your window and knock ever so gently.

The Legend of the Whispering Waters

By Patricia Matthews, Sarasota, Florida

The covered bridge at the Wakatomika River Girl Scout Camp in central Ohio is haunted with friendly spirits—so they say.

Legend tells of whispering waters. There were flint beds nearby and Indians often camped on the riverbanks while they mined flint needed for tools and arrows. In the evening, their voices drifted on the night air to other tribes camped there.

On a silent night, Girl Scout campers are told to listen for the voices and the call of the Indian spirit *Win-a-ba-shoo* asking for peace for all who gathered there.

A White Shapeless Mass Floated from the Bridge

By Shirley Ernst, Reading, Pennsylvania

Travelers at the turn of the century had a problem entering the Wertz's Red Covered Bridge in Pennsylvania after dark. When a buggy or wagon approached the entrance, the horses refused to enter—and no amount of coaxing would change their minds.

Word got around that the bridge was haunted, and travelers were cautioned to stay away. Eventually, however, a courageous man decided to walk through the bridge with his lantern to investigate.

As he entered the pitch-black bridge, he saw a white shapeless mass at the end of the bridge. It appeared to float from the bridge and disappear in the mist rising from the water below. His heart was pounding as he bravely advanced.

A second white form appeared as he made his way closer to the portal. Only this time he was able to drive the "ghost" away. You see, a number of white cows from a nearby dairy farm were using the bridge as a comfortable haven for the night!

Doris M. Soule

This Ghost Would Rather Keep His Identity Secret

Editor's Note: Many ghost stories grew out of shenanigans by mischievous boys. We received the following story and photo from a person who'd rather keep his identity secret—probably because he doesn't want his father to know he almost ruined their hayfork rope!

Some years ago, I lived near the covered bridge crossing Laurel Creek in Monroe County, West Virginia (at right). I had a buddy down the road, and his sister was going out on a date with her boyfriend. My buddy and I cooked up a plan to scare the couple as they walked home from their date.

We crawled up in the rafters of the bridge and suspended a sheet with a rope. We jiggled the sheet in ghostlike fashion as the couple approached in the darkness and waited for them to scream.

What we didn't know was the sister had gotten wind of the plan and had alerted her boyfriend to it. So as the couple neared the bridge, he said in a loud voice, "Just let me get my knife out. I'll fix that thing!"

Upon hearing that, our alarmed "ghost" seemed to yell out, "Don't cut! It's Poppy's good hayfork rope!"

123

Suddenly My Car Doors Locked Themselves

By Joetta Fredericks, Seymour, Connecticut

HAUNTED BRIDGE FANS. Joetta Fredericks (right) and daughter Wendy Picardo enjoyed visiting 139-foot Hammond Bridge, built by Asa Nourse in 1842.

While vacationing in Salisbury, Vermont, I bought some postcards, and one was of the Hammond Covered Bridge at nearby Pittsford.

"Hammond!" I exclaimed to my husband, David. "My great-grandfather, Jabez Hammond, was from Vermont. Do you suppose there's a connection?" Off we went to find the bridge on a lovely July morning.

When we located it, David took a walk across its length while I chatted with two workers from the plant up the road who were parked there having lunch. They were from Maine and couldn't tell me any of the history of the bridge.

As they drove off, I sat in our car with the passenger side door open so I could enjoy the sun and the butterflies flitting among the wildflowers. Suddenly the car door locks clicked shut…clicked open…then shut and opened once more. My first thought was that David was playing a trick on me with the car's keyless remote. But then I saw the key chain, with remote control attached, hanging from the ignition.

I'd just opened my mouth to tell this to David, when he blurted out, "I heard such strange noises on that bridge…like people talking and working. But I walked all the way to the end of the bridge, and no one was there."

Our daughter, Wendy, was intrigued with our story. So we made a return trip to the bridge a few days later. We also took my sister, Marie, with us. We thought *three* Hammond descendants might be powerful enough to ward off any ghosts! There were no uncanny incidents that day.

So what do you think? Could a radio signal have affected the door locks? Did the bridge act as a funnel for faraway noises? Or is Hammond Covered Bridge haunted?

Background photo: Olin/Dewey Road Covered Bridge, Ashtabula County, Ohio—Carl A. Stimac

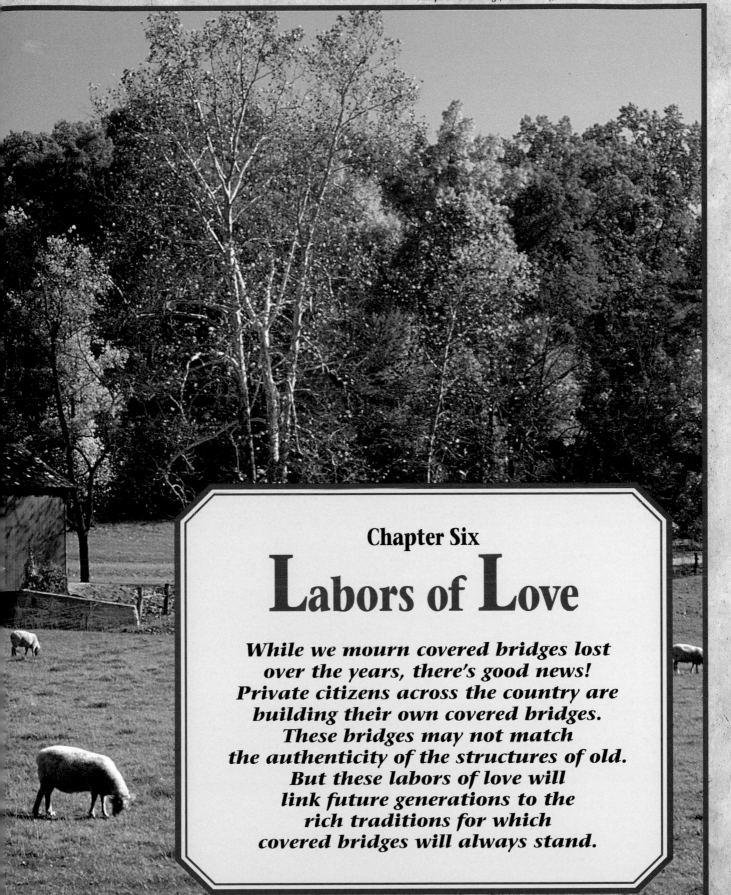

Chapter Six

Labors of Love

*While we mourn covered bridges lost
over the years, there's good news!
Private citizens across the country are
building their own covered bridges.
These bridges may not match
the authenticity of the structures of old.
But these labors of love will
link future generations to the
rich traditions for which
covered bridges will always stand.*

My Brother's Bridge Honors Our Parents

By Marilee McLaughlin, Medical Lake, Washington

My brother, Bernie Buck, built a covered bridge over a stream on his property near Puget Sound, Washington.

All the lumber used in Bernie's dream bridge—cedar, Douglas fir and western hemlock—was logged on the property and milled on-site. When it was finished, he dedicated the span to our mother and father, who were Kansas farmers.

The bridge provides a sheltered view of salmon returning each autumn to spawn in the stream 20 feet below.

Not only is my brother a bridge designer and builder, he is also the family poet laureate. He composed a poem (below) as he viewed his new bridge under a full moon from his bedroom window one evening.

A Bridge Builder's Prayer

Thank you, Lord, for this sylvan ridge
   With its moss-adorned stumps and stands of trees,
And for this view of an old-fashioned covered bridge
   Whose charm elicits all kinds of memories.

Reminiscent of times when a clop-clop-clop was
   The staccato serenade between "Giddyap!" and "Whoa!"
Back to the days when a blizzard couldn't stop
   The sleigh nor the buggy with its sleet and snow.

Back to the days when oats and hay
   Left us no need for foreign oil—
When horsepower spoke with a "whinny" and a "neigh"
   And their emissions were good for the soil.

They took us to both our church and our school,
   Standing side by side with their high-shingled steeples,
Where together they exhorted the Golden Rule
   With their Bible and their Primer teaching the people.

It takes us back to the days of the wiener roast,
   The ice cream social and the taffy pull,
To crock-churned butter on home-baked toast,
   To when a man could be content with his belly full.

It takes us back to the days of the crank telephone
   So elegantly mounted on the living room wall—
We were far from town, but never really alone,
   And no high-tech gadget ever recorded our call.

Yes, Lord, I do remember those days were hard—
   Our backs were sore and our hands were raw,
But we always felt safe in our own front yard
   And we seldom, if ever, needed help from the Law.

In fact, we seldom locked our home's front door—
   If it had been fitted with locks at all.
There was no reason to steal, everybody was poor.
   If a neighbor needed help, all he had to do was call.

Back then road rage was of no concern—
   We always waved at the passerby,
And we never experienced his threatening eye.

But in this age of space and speed,
   As the 20th century fades away,
More eight-lane bridges are not what we need.
   Help us get back to a quieter day.

   —Bernie Buck, Puget Sound, Washington

Grandkids Like to Play at 'Papa's Bridge'

By Evelyn Stites, Cookeville, Tennessee

"OUR FAMILY makes a big deal out of everything," says Evelyn. "We even had a ribbon-cutting ceremony when we completed our covered bridge."

We have three children, all of whom built their homes on our 800-acre farm. So we've had the joy of watching our 11 grandchildren grow up near us.

A creek runs through the farm, and two of our children built their homes on the other side of the creek. They drove through the water to go back and forth—until one morning after a heavy rain when our daughter-in-law stalled in the middle of the creek with her children in the car!

My husband, John, decided then and there it was time to build a bridge.

John built a covered bridge that we call Papa's Bridge. But it's more than a safe crossing over the creek—it's a gathering spot for our grandchildren. John built a room on top of the bridge where they could play and sleep out. He made a ladder attached to the wall of the bridge to access the room and a trapdoor in the floor...so when the door is closed, there is no danger of them falling out.

It has been fun listening to our grandchildren on the telephone saying to one another, "Meet you at the bridge." When John and I drive through the farm first thing in the morning and see bicycles and dogs waiting below, we know that some of them spent the night at Papa's Bridge.

Our family makes a "big deal" out of everything. So we had a dedication and picnic when the bridge was finished.

Every year since then on the Fourth of July, we set up picnic tables in the bridge to celebrate the wonderful country we live in. We have a barbecue pit nearby where we cook a whole pig, two 40-pound beef roasts, a goat, a lamb and chicken breasts. At noon, when the meat is ready, as many as 350 friends and family gather at the bridge for food and fellowship.

Papa's Bridge has given many wonderful memories to all of us!

Granddad's Bridge Had a Stormy Past

By Darlene Hunter, Corinth, Kentucky

We had to ford a stream to get to our new farm home built in 1986. At times, the water was too high and too swift to cross safely, so we began preparations to build a bridge.

We were toying with the idea of a covered bridge when my husband, Gary, remembered the old covered bridge that had burned around 1953 at the nearby community of Natlee, Kentucky. As a child, Gary had lived across the road from that bridge. He still remembers being awakened in the wee hours of the morning and watching the bridge burn.

The Natlee Covered Bridge was built in 1874. It was special to Gary because his grandfather, Hillary Hunter Sr., helped repair the bridge some years later when the original beams needed to be replaced. After the fire, the beams that remained from Granddad's handiwork were pulled to a nearby farm, where they lay long forgotten.

Gary called the owner of the farm, and we were able to purchase those beams. They are now in our covered bridge, which we built in 1990.

The turbulent times were not over for our bridge, however. The flood of 1997 washed it off its footings and floated it downstream. Luckily, it washed

into a small river bottom, where some trees prevented it from washing away.

We were able to pull the bridge back to our farm with a tractor by rolling it on logs. It was a slow process, but we praise the Lord that it was not too damaged to restore.

We are so happy to have our covered bridge back—particularly so our two grandchildren can enjoy the role their great-great-grandfather played in this piece of history.

I Built My Bridge *After* I Fixed Up Her Kitchen

By Kenny Johnson, Bronson, Iowa

I had wanted a covered bridge for years. But my wife, Susan, had other ideas—she insisted on getting a new kitchen first. So putting my priorities in order, I remodeled the kitchen!

Then I was finally able to build my covered bridge. It's part of our driveway that runs between two ponds. It's 14 feet wide and 36 feet long. It's also wired for electricity, so we're able to plug in Christmas lights and turn on a lighted display of Santa and his sleigh and reindeer that we mount on the roof.

There's a windmill nearby that pumps water from an 88-foot-deep well into the small pond by the bridge. From there the water flows via a flower-lined spillway into the larger pond.

To complete the landscape, Susan planted a flower bed that's 5 feet wide and 250 feet long and filled with annuals and perennials.

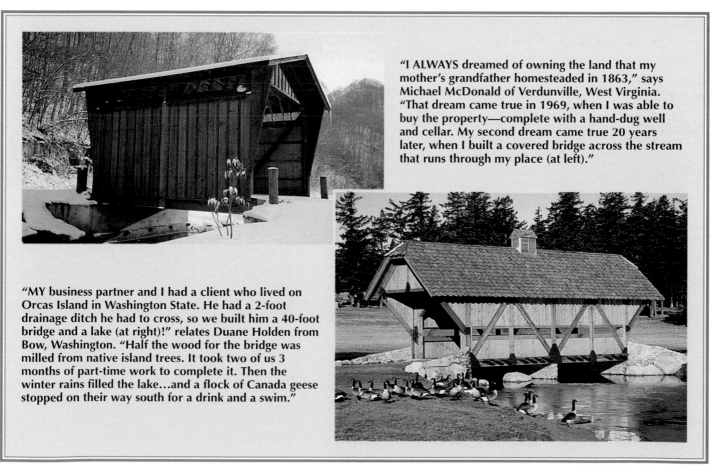

"I ALWAYS dreamed of owning the land that my mother's grandfather homesteaded in 1863," says Michael McDonald of Verdunville, West Virginia. "That dream came true in 1969, when I was able to buy the property—complete with a hand-dug well and cellar. My second dream came true 20 years later, when I built a covered bridge across the stream that runs through my place (at left)."

"MY business partner and I had a client who lived on Orcas Island in Washington State. He had a 2-foot drainage ditch he had to cross, so we built him a 40-foot bridge and a lake (at right)!" relates Duane Holden from Bow, Washington. "Half the wood for the bridge was milled from native island trees. It took two of us 3 months of part-time work to complete it. Then the winter rains filled the lake...and a flock of Canada geese stopped on their way south for a drink and a swim."

Georgia Bridge Spreads Christmas Cheer

By Jackie Whitehead, Lincolnton, Georgia

My favorite covered bridge leads to a very special place in my heart—my home near Lincolnton, Georgia.

The driveway to our house winds its way about a quarter of a mile past beautiful trees and farmland. We built the bridge to cross a small pond in front of the house. It's 12 feet wide and 46 feet long and has open areas and 10 windows from which you can stop and look out over the pond.

The bridge was dedicated with a celebration on July 4, 1995. We decorated it with red, white and blue and invited family and friends for a barbecue.

Soon after that gathering, Dad began planning ways to celebrate Christmas. With the family pitching in, "Christmas at the Covered Bridge" was born—and it has become an annual event in our community of 9,000.

Early in November, we get out the decorations and transform the bridge into a Christmas wonderland. White lights outline the bridge, and yards and yards of garland surround each window. The windows come alive with animated scenes of Noah's Ark, skaters, elves, trains, angels, dolls and, most importantly, the Nativity. Christmas carols and the laughter of children fill the air.

Each evening from the Saturday after Thanksgiving through the Christmas holidays, members of our family sit around a fire and greet visitors as they arrive to view the bridge. After they've seen the display, we invite them to join us for hot chocolate and roasted marshmallows.

Christmas at the Covered Bridge started out as a way for our family to celebrate Christmas. But it has grown into a wonderful way to share the sweet spirit of the season with the community. In 1997, we estimated 3,000 visitors viewed the bridge.

Our covered bridge is a blessing to our family—bringing us together and enabling us to meet many new friends.

"THESE ARE some snapshots of the Christmas festivities at our covered bridge," explains Jackie. "In 1997, we hosted about 3,000 people!"

My Dad's Covered Bridge

By Susan Speth, Marshfield, Wisconsin

My dad, Bill Haas, has been fascinated with covered bridges most of his life and always dreamed of building his own one day. So whenever he and Mom went to covered bridge festivals, they'd take photos and study the construction inside and out.

In 1990, my brothers started taking over the family business. That's when Dad found the time to build "his bridge" over the pond on his land in Wood County, Wisconsin.

The bridge is 34 feet long. Dad did most of the work in November and December. This made the final stages of construction easier since he could stand on the ice while he worked. Then the following summer, he painted the bridge red.

Since Dad built his bridge, many people have come to see and photograph it. His grandchildren pretend there's a troll under it and play "billy goats gruff" and many made-up games. At Christmastime, he decorates it festively with lights (right).

It took long years for Dad's dream to become reality. Now it brings enjoyment to many people.

"A STREAM separates our land and the land owned by my husband's brother, Stuart. So with financial help from their mother, Cecile, my husband, Jeff, and Stuart built a covered bridge to permanently connect our two homes," explains Margaret Davis of Westfield, Illinois. "We invited all of our family and friends from our little village of Westfield to help dedicate the bridge. At the dedication, a plaque was presented to Cecile and then hung in the bridge. It reads: 'This bridge was built by two brothers as a symbol of love between our families and in honor of our mother, Cecile Goble. May it always be crossed in that spirit. Stu and Jeff Davis, June 1994.'"

There's a Wedding at Our Bridge Almost Every Weekend!

By Marilyn and Virgil Lovitt, Sharonville, Ohio

When we built our home, there was one problem—the driveway ran literally through a creek. We had to drive through the water across a concrete ford.

We knew we'd have to build a bridge, so why not make it a covered bridge? We've visited covered bridges all over the United States as well as in several foreign countries. There may be some covered bridges that we haven't seen in the last 45 years... but not many! So we designed our bridge from what we thought were the best features of all that we had seen.

The flower boxes on each side were an idea from the well-known covered bridge in Lucerne, Switzerland. We have four different types of silk flowers for these boxes and change them with the seasons.

At Christmastime, we string the bridge with lights and prop two huge toy soldiers at its entrance. We also arrange lights in the outline of a horse and surrey on the side of the bridge—including traveling lights that appear to make the horse's feet move and the wheels on the carriage turn.

Our bridge is used almost every weekend from May to November for weddings or wedding photos. All we ask is that the bride and groom send us a picture of them on the bridge to add to our growing wedding album!

The bridge has also been used for family reunions, a senior citizen lunch, a family rummage sale and even a stop for a Model A Ford road rally.

THIS COUPLE is one of the many that are married at the Lovitts' covered bridge each year.

"LIZ'S BRIDGE (at right) was built in 1997 over the Pequonnock River by town employees at the entrance to our community's Twin Brooks Park," relates Elizabeth Smith of Trumbull, Connecticut, who spent many years garnering support for the project. "I cannot begin to tell you how thrilled and surprised I was at the bridge dedication to learn that they named the bridge for me. I think this is the most wonderful, beautiful, awesome bridge there ever was!"

"MY HUSBAND, Ken, and I own 60 acres of timberland with a stream running through it—a perfect spot for a covered bridge," comments Linda Rowell of Nikolaevsk, Alaska. "The bridge (at left) is 24 feet long and was completed in 1994. We call it 'Bill's Bridge' after a dear friend who died suddenly while we were building it. In 1996, we constructed our dream retirement home overlooking the creek. Ken's next dream is to build a working gristmill along the creek."

Life Slows Down When We Drive Across Our Bridge

By Ruby Davis, Newark, Ohio

On a small county road in rural Licking County, Ohio, there's a covered bridge that's near and dear to our hearts. The locals recognize it as the Davis Covered Bridge.

Spanning the Rocky Fork Creek, the bridge (pictured below) measures a mere 50 feet, but it was built with love and care by my husband, Harry, and his father and uncle back in 1948. It's the only access to our farm. In 1990, we enlisted the help of two Amish men to make some needed repairs. The covered bridge has withstood floods and heavy snows blanketing the rooftop. It has held up to the weight of countless cars, trucks, farm machinery and wagons loaded with hay.

Harry fondly remembers riding his horse through the bridge again and again as a boy just to hear the horse's hooves beating against the wood of the bridge floor. The bridge was once a safe haven for our daughters caught in a snowstorm...and a chapel for their make-believe weddings in the summertime.

The Davis Covered Bridge is a source of pride for my husband and me as well as our children and grandchildren. It's our hope that our little piece of history will be remembered and enjoyed for generations to come.

In this fast-paced age, it's nice to know that we can pull across our bridge at the end of the day and feel, for just a moment, time slip back to a slower pace.

"A STREAM runs through our property, and on the other side, we have a campfire site, picnic area and a place to play horseshoes," says Deborah Myers of Wakeman, Ohio. "To get across the stream, my husband, Stephen, and I built a covered bridge (at left). It's our pride and joy."

"SOME people have a home on a lake where they can get away to relax. We have a covered bridge!" shares Arlene Haarsma of Hartley, Iowa. "We built our covered bridge (below) on an old railroad trestle bridge about a half mile from our home. It's 70 feet long and constructed from an old barn we dismantled. The 'sunset side' of the bridge has a large picture window and two stained glass windows, and the 'sunrise side' has five windows. We built tables and chairs inside, and our family enjoys picnics several times a week there. We also built a cabin nearby and call our getaway Trestle Park."

"IN THE summer of 1997, my husband, Ken, built a riding arena in the woods on the other side of the creek from our barn," relates Brenda Wyant of Cuba, New York. "We've always had a passion for covered bridges, and since we needed a bridge to get to the arena, we decided to build a covered one. It's 26 feet long and 10 feet wide and made of hemlock and oak (at left). We don't have any problems getting the horses to cross the bridge, and what a wonderful sound their hooves make on the bridge."

"WE NEEDED ACCESS to the site for our new home along the Calaveras River and spent several years researching covered bridges before our vision of the Becker Bridge (at left) became a reality in 1996," note Garrett and Renee Becker of Linden, California. "The setting for our home is a beautiful small farm community surrounded by orchards, lush foliage and the sound of the water flowing underneath our bridge. It's a real hideaway."

"AFTER TOURING New England to see the fall foliage and covered bridges, I told my husband, Darrell, I'd like a covered bridge for Christmas," relates Daphne Flurry of Jasper, Texas. "The bridge (at right) was the best Christmas gift I have ever received. I hope my children and grandchildren will enjoy it in the years to come as much as I have."

"MY SON, Jared, and his wife, Becca, built Hickory Grove Covered Bridge (at left) on 11 acres near Canton, Pennsylvania where they plan to build a log home," shares Bobbee Wilcox, also of Canton. "He's an English teacher who loves to build things. The bridge is 30 feet long and was made with lumber from a neighbor's old barn that had collapsed. It has given our family immeasurable pleasure as we cross it to attend family picnics and marshmallow roasts. A screech owl gave its approval by taking up residence in the bridge rafters last fall."

Don't Forget to Sign Our Guest Book

By Mark Gabrick, Lake Ann, Michigan

We bought a beautiful 22-acre parcel of land on Michigan's Lake Ann in 1994. The property featured huge trees, a creek and wonderful lake frontage. There was only one problem—the creek ran through a 20-foot-wide ravine, which made three-fourths of our land difficult to access.

I was planning to build a simple bridge to cross the ravine when an engineer friend suggested I make it a covered bridge. Since I owned a sawmill, this sounded like a good idea.

First, we had to wade through the red tape of getting permits and approvals. Next, there were roads to build and footings to be dug. We poured concrete footings and supports, which we covered with fieldstone for aesthetic purposes.

The main structure is actually steel, built to support a 100,000-pound load. Once it was in place, we bolted down white oak deck planks 2-1/2 inches thick. We built a simple post-and-beam structure over the deck and covered the roof with split-cedar shingles. My father-in-law made a stainless steel cross that hangs from one end of the bridge so God can look down upon this creation.

We named the bridge "Joshua's Crossing" for our son. There is a short road leading to the bridge, which we named "Tasha's Trail" after our daughter, Natasha.

We feel God has blessed us with this bridge and hope that it will also bless others. So if you're ever visiting Lake Ann, remember to look for Tasha's Trail. It will lead you to Joshua's Crossing. Be sure to sign the guest book!

"WE USED split cedar shingles on the roof of our bridge to give it a rustic look," explains Mark (at top with his son Joshua).

We're Making New Memories On Granddaddy's Bridge

By Jana Mayo, Gallant, Alabama

My parents recently moved into the house where my mother grew up.

One of the things that makes the place so special is the covered bridge that my granddaddy, Chester, built. It stretches over a pond and is part of a driveway that leads to the house.

I can remember playing on the bridge as a child—usually while my brother and my cousin were fishing. I also remember them sliding on the ice all the way under the bridge when the pond was frozen over. (I was too afraid to try it.)

When I married, I had my wedding pictures taken at the bridge. With my husband and me in white, the blue water of the pond, the bright sunshine and the red covered bridge in the background, our pictures turned out beautifully.

Now we're making new bridge memories. We live nearby in the house where I grew up. So my son, Tanner, is able to wake up every morning and see the bridge just like I did. He and my dad enjoy taking the wagon across the bridge to feed the fish.

I'm proud to be part of the history of our family's covered bridge and think of my granddaddy whenever I look at it.

MEMORIES LIVE ON. Jana and Jim Mayo (left) were married near Jana's granddad's bridge. Their son, Tanner, and his grandpa, Charles Bryson, find the bridge a convenient wagon crossing (above).

"I ALWAYS wanted to build a covered bridge but couldn't afford the lumber on my retirement income," says Mark Stephens of Mt. Vernon, Ohio. "Several years went by, and my cousin had a 150-year-old barn with oak timbers that he wanted torn down. I finally had my lumber! A friend drew up the plans and also gave me wood shingles from our old church roof. As you can see from the photo (at left), we like to decorate the bridge at Christmastime for all to enjoy."

"MY husband, John, and I purchased part of an old family farm along Two Mile Creek where milk cows had once been pastured," explains Carlene Cochran of Kane, Pennsylvania. "John built a bridge to provide access to our new property, and after completing it, he thought it would be a pretty setting for a covered bridge. So a few years later, he added the roof and sides. The bridge planks are not nailed down, so they rumble when we drive across them. It's a sound we both love because it brings back memories of covered bridges that have been replaced by concrete and steel."

"MY WIFE and I are retired and live on 40 wooded acres in the Upper Pennisula of Michigan," writes Gerald Beaudoin of Stephenson. "We have a fish pond and numerous trails through the woods on which our grandchildren enjoy riding golf carts. We built this bridge over a ditch to give us access to other trails—and to beautify our yard. We designed it to also provide storage in the winter. So we built doors on both ends and shutters to close the openings that run the entire length of the bridge. The window is leaded glass from my parents' house and about 90 years old."

We Have Seven Covered Bridges!

By Ellis Barrett, Keene, New Hampshire

I love the nostalgic appearance, historic charm and purposeful structure of covered bridges. In fact, I appreciate them so much that we have seven of them on our 36-hole Bretwood Golf Course near Keene, New Hampshire.

Five of these bridges span the Ashuelot River, which winds through the course. Two smaller bridges cross swale areas on the course.

The coverings help to preserve the superstructures from the harsh New England weather. The bridges, ranging in length from 65 feet to 90 feet, also serve as shelters for golfers caught in a sudden thunderstorm.

"THIS COVERED BRIDGE was built by my husband in 1994, when he was 72 years old," writes Virginia Aloia of West Finley, Pennsylvania. "He's gone now, but we spent many evenings sitting on our swing inside the bridge."

"THE PEOPLE of Cook, Nebraska, population 335, built this covered bridge in 1989," says Elmer Armknecht Sr. of Auburn. "It's one of the reasons why this progressive community was judged 'Best Little Town in America' in 1992."

We Built This Bridge for Our Grandchildren...and Their Grandchildren

By Mel and Dolores Biggs, Dallas, Texas

Our covered bridge began as a simple footbridge spanning a creek that bisects our East Texas farm. After one of our grandchildren tumbled 14 feet from the bridge to the creek bed (shaken, but unharmed), we decided safety measures were in order. So we built a covered bridge.

We decided to incorporate some history into our bridge, even though it was just recently built in 1993. The cupola on top and the chandelier inside were salvaged from a home once occupied by a former governor of Texas. The beams are timbers scavenged from various old buildings—with the exception of the steel girders that make it sturdy enough to drive our farm tractor across.

The inside walls are covered with old cedar fencing arranged in a herringbone pattern. A small wooden cross adorns the peak of the gable on each end to remind us where our many blessings come from.

The bridge is also a museum of sorts. There are antique tools, farm implements, household items, etc. mounted on the walls. We're presently collecting old auto license plates from each state we've visited. And friends often bring us items to include in our display.

We hope the bridge will remain for our grandchildren and their grandchildren to enjoy...and that they'll add their own chapters to the story of our covered bridge.

143

My Neighbors Think I'm a Little Nuts

By David Brunner, Colden Valley, New York

After building a bridge in our backyard to carry our tractor and lawn mower across a ravine, I decided to turn it into a covered bridge.

The thinking and design stage took about 3 years. I actually constructed the covered portions in the summers of 1996 and 1997.

I attempted to make it look as authentic as possible by using cedar shingles on the roof and sides to cover the plywood sheathing. I installed carriage lamps on the ends and some old green pool table reflector lamps inside the peak to flood the interior with light.

Some of my neighbors think I'm a little nuts. But one neighbor thinks the bridge looks so neat with the lights on that he asks us to light it whenever he hosts a party!

"MY HUSBAND, John, built this covered bridge over the creek that runs through our property," explains Mary Ann Miller of Sturgis, Michigan. "He put a lot of hard work and love into building it and then named it after me. So it's my special bridge."

"OUR COVERED BRIDGE crosses Park Creek in the town of Kirkwood, New York and is the pedestrian gateway to the Kirkwood Valley Park," explains Ken Newberry of Kirkwood. "The bridge was built in 1997 with great pride by employees of the town with lumber from a local sawmill."

We Built a Bridge to Cover Up an Ugly Ditch

By Cora Smith
Frankfort, New York

Our county decided to dig a ditch along our road in June 1996. I've lived in our house for almost 70 years, and it was traumatic, to say the least, to see huge machinery scoop out an ugly 5-foot-deep by 8-foot-wide trench in what used to be our front yard.

My husband, Ed, loves the challenge of building something no one else would think of. So he quickly decided to improve the looks of the ditch by spanning it with a covered bridge. He hoped not only to detract from the ugliness of the ditch, but to also provide a place for our mailbox and a mailbox for our neighbor across the road.

When Ed saw the ditch digger coming up the road in June, he started sketching his design. By late August, the bridge was completed. He even constructed our mailbox with front and back doors, so we could remove our mail from the back without stepping onto the road.

One of our bridge's most enthusiastic fans was our daughter. When she saw ours, she wanted her dad to build a covered bridge across the ditch in front of her house. He completed it just in time for her to decorate it for Christmas.

Bartlett Covered Bridge, North Conway, New Hampshire—Photo: Ray Packard

Wilkinson Pioneer Park Covered Bridge, Rock Falls, Iowa—Photo: Ty Smedes

"OUR COVERED BRIDGE crosses Park Creek in the town of Kirkwood, New York and is the pedestrian gateway to the Kirkwood Valley Park," explains Ken Newberry of Kirkwood. "The bridge was built in 1997 with great pride by employees of the town with lumber from a local sawmill."

We Built a Bridge to Cover Up an Ugly Ditch

By Cora Smith
Frankfort, New York

Our county decided to dig a ditch along our road in June 1996. I've lived in our house for almost 70 years, and it was traumatic, to say the least, to see huge machinery scoop out an ugly 5-foot-deep by 8-foot-wide trench in what used to be our front yard.

My husband, Ed, loves the challenge of building something no one else would think of. So he quickly decided to improve the looks of the ditch by spanning it with a covered bridge. He hoped not only to detract from the ugliness of the ditch, but to also provide a place for our mailbox and a mailbox for our neighbor across the road.

When Ed saw the ditch digger coming up the road in June, he started sketching his design. By late August, the bridge was completed. He even constructed our mailbox with front and back doors, so we could remove our mail from the back without stepping onto the road.

One of our bridge's most enthusiastic fans was our daughter. When she saw ours, she wanted her dad to build a covered bridge across the ditch in front of her house. He completed it just in time for her to decorate it for Christmas.

I Gave My Wife a Bridge for Our Anniversary

By Jim Hern, Pickerington, Ohio

We seem to yearn for a simpler time. A time when the days were longer and nights were quieter. A time when summers would drag lazily on for what seemed an eternity and winters meant snowfall and warm cozy fires crackling away in the fireplace. We long for the times when our families would tell stories about how life was in the early years. Whatever happened to those times? Where did the good ol' days go? We are all so fast-paced these days. Our world is getting smaller. It's strange that just a few years ago, a person would have to actually go someplace to know what it looked like. And now you can see places in front of you that you never dreamed possible. Someday, maybe we will be able to get back to the basics. Generally speaking, people are resisting the change of modern society. I am going to make a resolution for this next year to look back to the less pressured days of the past and to make every effort to keep the knowledge of simple days alive in my heart and share it with family and friends.
—*Alonzo Hern*
30th day of December, 1919

I decided to share this excerpt from my great-great-grandfather's journal (left) to illustrate how some things haven't changed. Sometimes we spend so much time looking for the good old days that we overlook the day we are living!

Even though I'm sitting in my climate-controlled house, with my digital pager at my side, a cellular phone at arm's reach and a compact disc player projecting soft music in the background, the fact is that 50 years from now, someone will reminisce about this era...and call it the "good ol' days"!

Instead of simply longing for the past, I believe we must make new memories every day. It's our responsibility to create stories that our children can tell their children. Here's one I hope they tell over and over again:

Seven years ago, I was courting my sweetheart, Jodi. A Jeep was our buggy, and country roads were the backdrop for our adventures. We leisurely drove through the countryside and stopped at old schoolhouses, scenic hilltop views and, our favorite of all, covered bridges.

It didn't matter what the weather was because the covered bridges sheltered us. On rainy spring days, we'd stand inside the old bridges and listen to the soft whisper of the raindrops on the roof. Some of the roofs were covered with slate shingles and others with wood shingles. Each bridge made its own song.

Piece by Piece

Our trips through the country kindled a love between us. Just like a finely built bridge, timber by timber, we were constructing a union between two lifestyles— joining the shores of our lives.

It doesn't cost anything to visit covered bridges, so I was able to secretly save money to buy an engagement ring. It was fall, and the nights were getting longer and cooler.

Jodi was finishing her college education and had to drop off a final exam at The Ohio University/Lancaster branch. The John Bright No. 2 Covered Bridge, newly restored and lighted at night, was on campus. It was the perfect atmosphere for my plans.

My girl was a little reluctant to walk across the dark field, wet with the evening dew, to reach the bridge that night. But I had already asked her father for her hand in marriage, and I had the ring in my pocket. So I was not about to let this opportunity pass! Finally, she agreed to go.

There Was One Hang-Up

By the time we reached the bridge, I'd gone over the script in my mind a thousand times—I was ready to pop the question. But when we got there, I couldn't believe my eyes. I had envisioned us being alone under the moonlight and stars. But there on the other end of the bridge stood another couple. Jodi thought we should leave and not offend them, but I was determined to out-stay them!

After what seemed an eternity, they drifted into the darkness. That's when I walked my sweetheart to the center of the bridge, knelt down on one

knee and asked her if she would make me the happiest man on earth by marrying me. She graced me with a tearful yes.

We were married on September 7, 1991. We continued our trips to covered bridges after our marriage. So in 1996, I wanted to recognize our fifth wedding anniversary with a gift of a covered bridge. You see, the recommended gift for a fifth anniversary is wood!

I began searching for a covered bridge that I could buy and move to the stream behind our house. But I found very little available and a lot of red tape. So I drew up plans and began to build my own bridge in July of that year. On Friday, September 6, I drove the last nail into the bridge, and it was ready for our anniversary the next day.

We had a big party to celebrate. The weather was perfect, and we finished off the evening with a good old-fashioned bonfire.

Our bridge is a celebration of love and the symbol of our relationship. A plaque on it reads, "The Hern Bridge, a bridge that joins two shores."

Let the memories begin!

Bartlett Covered Bridge, North Conway, New Hampshire—Photo: Ray Packard

Wilkinson Pioneer Park Covered Bridge, Rock Falls, Iowa—Photo: Ty Smedes

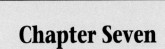

Chapter Seven

Just the Facts

Want to learn more? The following pages are a resource guide of places you can go for more information...plus other tidbits to add to your enjoyment next time you cross a covered bridge.

Mansfield Gristmill and Covered Bridge,
Parke County, Indiana—Photo: Marsha Williamson Mohr

Bridge at the Green, West Arlington, Vermont—Photo: Mae Scanlan

Organizations

National Society for the Preservation of Covered Bridges, Davis Topham, Treasurer, 1021 Cellana Ct., Ft. Myers FL 33908-1606 (November-April); 50 Samoset Village Way, Rockport ME 04856-9501 (May-October). Phone 1-207/596-7472. Publication: *Covered Bridge Topics*, quarterly newsletter. Membership rates: $15 for individuals, $5 for students.

The Bridge Covered, 110 Shady Ln., Fayetteville NY 13066.

Indiana—Parke County Convention and Visitors Bureau, P.O. Box 165, Rockville IN 47872-0165. Phone 1-765/569-5226. To receive the Parke County Guide to the Covered Bridge Festival, write Parke County Guide, 20 South Jackson St., Greencastle IN 46135 or call 1-765/653-4026

Indiana—Rush County Heritage Inc., Larry Stout, President, 6352W 650S, Rushville IN 46173. Phone 1-765/629-2892.

Indiana Covered Bridge Society, John Sechrist, Treasurer, 725 Sanders St., Indianapolis IN 46203.

Kentucky Covered Bridge Association, 62 Miami Pkwy., Ft. Thomas KY 41075-1137. Phone 1-606/441-7000. Fax 1-606/441-2112. Internet address: lkpatton@fuse.net. Publication: *Timber Tunnel Talk*, contains information on bridges in Kentucky and elsewhere. Membership rates: from $9 annually.

Maryland—Frederick County Covered Bridge Preservation Society, P.O. Box 143, Thurmont MD 21788.

Minnesota—Zumbrota Covered Bridge Association, 17326-420th St., Zumbrota MN 55992-5028. Or contact Alma Swanson, 7124 River Shore Ln., Champlin MN 55316.

New Hampshire—Langdon, New Hampshire Covered Bridge Association, R.R. 1, Box 123A, Langdon NH 03602. Phone 1-603/835-6844.

New York State Covered Bridge Society, 6342 Martin Dr., Rome NY 13440. Or contact Henry Messing, Treasurer, 958 Grove St., Elmira NY 14901. Publication: T*he Empire State Courier*, details covered bridges in New York.

Ohio Historic Bridge Association, 3155 Whitehead Rd., Columbus OH

43204-1855. Publication: *Bridges & Byways*, quarterly newsletter spotlighting the historic bridges of Ohio.

Ohio—Ashtabula County Covered Bridge Committee, Betty Morrisson, Ashtabula County Courthouse Building, 25 West Jefferson St., Jefferson OH 44047. Phone 1-440/576-3769.

Ohio—Northern Ohio Covered Bridge Society, 642 Firestone Blvd., Akron OH 44306. Or contact Pat Eierman, 6622 Balsam Dr., Bedford Heights OH 44146. Publication: *Buckeye Bridge Briefs*.

Oregon—Covered Bridge Society of Oregon, 24595 S.W. Neill Rd., Sherwood OR 97140. Phone 1-503/628-1906. Or contact Bill Cockrell, 3940 Courtney Ln. SE, Salem OR 97302. Publication: *The Bridge Tender*, quarterly newsletter on West Coast covered bridges.

Pennsylvania—Bucks County Conference and Visitors Bureau Inc., 152 Swamp Rd., Doylestown PA 18901-2451. Phone 1-800/836-2825.

Pennsylvania—Theodore Burr Covered Bridge Society of Pennsylvania Inc., P.O. Box 2383, Lancaster PA 17603-2383. Or contact Russel Holmes, Treasurer, Box 95, Seven Valleys PA 17360-0095, or Thomas Walczak, President, 3012 Old Pittsburg Rd., New Castle PA 16101-6085. Publications: *Pennsylvania Crossing*, a report on activities and events related to covered bridges in Pennsylvania, and *Wooden Covered Spans*, an overview of covered bridge affairs throughout the country.

Pennsylvania—Bedford County Visitors Bureau, R.D. 1, Box 44, Everett PA 15537. Contact Walter Cox, Bedford Shopper's Guide, 100 Masters Ave., Everett PA 15537, or call Bedford County Visitors Bureau at 1-800/765-3331. Internet address: www.bedfordcounty.netforwardbridges.

Pennsylvania—The Keystone Grange Covered Bridge Society, P.O. Box 311, Collegeville PA 19426.

Quebec—Le Societe Quebecoise Des Ponts Couverts Inc., 2126 De Lorimier, Longueuil PQ Canada J4K 3N9.

Virginia—Office of Public Affairs, Virginia Department of Transportation, 1401 E. Broad St., Richmond VA 23219. Phone 1-804/786-5731.

Festivals

Alabama—Blount County Covered Bridge Festival, fourth weekend in October. Contact Blount County-Oneonta Chamber of Commerce, P.O. Box 87, Oneonta AL 35121. Phone 1-205/274-2153.

Indiana—Cumberland Covered Bridge Festival, held annually. Contact the Matthews Lions Club, Box 55, Matthews IN 46957.

Indiana—Moscow Covered Bridge Festival, Moscow, Rush County, Indiana. Contact Jolene Icenogle, 1-765/629-2468, or Janice Hoban, 1-765/629-2427.

Indiana—Parke County Covered Bridge Festival. Contact Parke County Convention and Visitors Bureau, P.O. Box 165, Rockville IN 47872-0165. Phone 1-317/569-5226.

Iowa—Madison County Covered Bridge Festival. Contact Madison County Chamber of Commerce, 73 Jefferson St., Winterset IA 50273.

New Hampshire—Newport's Covered Bridge and Arts Festival, held annually the last week of September. Contact Newport Historical Society, P.O. Box 413, Newport NH 03773.

Ohio—Ashtabula County Covered Bridge Festival, held annually the second weekend of October at the fairgrounds in Jefferson. Contact Covered Bridge Festival Office, 25 W. Jefferson St., Jefferson OH 44047. Phone 1-216/576-3769.

Ohio—Greene County Covered Bridge Tour, contact Greene County Convention and Visitors Bureau, 3335 East Peterson Rd., Beavercreek OH 45430. Phone 1-513/429-9100 or 1-800/733-9109.

Pennsylvania—Annual Covered Bridge and Arts Festival. Contact Columbia-Montour Tourist Promotion Agency, 121 Papermill Rd., Bloomsburg PA 17815. Phone 1-717/784-8279 or 1-800/847-4810.

Pennsylvania—Covered Bridge Festival in Greene and Washington Counties. Contact Washington County Tourism and Promotion Agency, P.O. Box 877, 59 N. Main St., Washington PA 15301. Phone 1-412/222-8130 or 1-800/531-4114.

Pennsylvania—Tracking Covered Bridges in the Lehigh Valley, a self-guided tour. Contact the Lehigh Valley Convention and Visitors Bureau, P.O. Box 20785, Lehigh Valley PA 18002-0785. Phone 1-610/882-9200.

Books and Guides—By State

CONNECTICUT
Covered Bridges of Connecticut by Andrew Howard, The Village Press, Unionville CT, 1985.

GEORGIA
Georgia's Romantic Bridges, Public Information Office, Georgia Department of Transportation, circa 1980.

ILLINOIS, IOWA AND WISCONSIN
Covered Bridges in Illinois, Iowa and Wisconsin by Leslie Swanson, 1960; new edition, 1970.

INDIANA
Indiana Covered Bridges Thru the Years by George Gould, Indiana Covered Bridge Society Inc., Indianapolis IN, 1977.

The Covered Bridges of Indiana by Max Harvey, Wabash Valley Printing Co., Montezuma IN, 1966.

The Covered Bridges of Parke County by Max Harvey, Wabash Valley Printing Co., Montezuma IN, 1963.

Way Back When—Informal Essays from Rush County Oral History, Indiana Junior Historical Society, Indianapolis IN, circa 1981.

Indiana Covered Bridge Location Guide by Arthur Gatewood Jr.

The Covered Bridges of Parke County, Indiana by Wayne Weber.

Covered Bridges of the Byways of Indiana by Bryan Ketcham.

Covered Bridges of Indiana by Wayne Weber.

Bridges of the Past, Historic Landmarks of Parke County by Bob McElwee.

IOWA
Covered Bridges in Iowa by William Peterson, The Palimpsest, The State Historical Society of Iowa, Iowa City IA, Vol. LI, No. 11, November 1970.

KENTUCKY
Covered Bridges, Focus on Kentucky by Vernon White.

MAINE
Old Covered Bridges of Maine by Adelbert Jakeman, Sea Haven, Ocean Park ME, second printing, 1980.

Maine Covered Bridge Finder by E.B. Robertson and D.K. Roberson.

MARYLAND
Covered Bridges in Maryland by Judy E. Melvin Edelheit.

MASSACHUSETTS
Covered Bridges of Massachusetts by Andrew Howard, The Village Press, Unionville CT, 1978.

MICHIGAN
The Building of Zehnder's Holz-Brucke by Milton Graton, Clifford-Nicol Inc., Plymouth NH, 1980.

MISSOURI
Missouri Mills and Covered Bridges, The Missouri Tourism Commission, Jefferson City MO, circa 1972.

NEW HAMPSHIRE
50 Old Bridges of Lebanon, New Hampshire by Bernard Chapman and Robert Leavitt, The Lebanon Historical Society, 1975.

New Hampshire Covered Bridges—A Link With Our Past, by Richard Marshall, TDS Printing, Nashua NH, 1994.

New Hampshire's Covered Bridges by Stan Snow and Thedia Cox Ken-yon, Wake-Brook House, Sanbornville NH, 1957.

Spanning Time: New Hampshire Covered Bridges by Irene DuPont.

NEW JERSEY
Of Time, Fire and the River—The Story of New Jersey's Covered Bridges by Norman Brydon, August 1971.

NEW YORK
Guide to the Covered Bridges of New York State by Stott Anderson, 1962.

Spans of Time—Covered Bridges of Delaware County, New York by Ward Herrman, Delside Press, Delhi NY 1974.

Timbers of Time—The Existing Covered Bridges of Ulster County by Patricia Bartels Miller, The Erpf Catskill Cultural Center Inc., Arkville NY, 1977.

Some Delaware County Bridges by Margaret Turnbull, Delaware County History, Fall 1974, Vol. 6, The Delaware County Historical Association.

Blenheim Covered Bridge—125th Anniversary, North Blenheim NY, 1980.

OHIO
Covered Bridges of Preble County, Ohio by Seth Schlotterbeck, The Preble County Historical Society, 7693 Swartsel Rd., Eaton OH 45320; 1976.

Muskingum River Covered Bridges by Norris Schneider, Southern Ohio Covered Bridge Association Inc., Zanesville OH 1971.

The Covered Bridges of Ohio by Miriam Wood, The Old Trail Printing Co., Columbus OH, 1993.

Covered Bridge Pictoral Review, Ashtabula County Historical Society, Vol. 15, No. 1, March 1968.

Life in the Slow Lane: Fifty Backroad Tours of Ohio by Jeff and Nadean Disabato Traylor

OREGON
Roofs Over Rivers—A Guide to Oregon's Covered Bridges by Nick and Bill Cockrell, The Touchstone Press, Beaverton OR, 1978. Send $8 with request to Bill Cockrell, 3940 Courtney Ln. SE, Salem OR 97302.

A Century of Oregon Covered Bridges 1851-1952 by Lee H. Nelson, Oregon Historical Society, Portland OR, 1960.

Guide to Covered Bridges in Albany Area, Albany Visitors Association, P.O. Box 965, Albany OR 97321. Phone 1-800/526-2256.

Guide to Covered Bridges in Lane County, Eugene-Springfield Convention and Visitors Bureau, P.O. Box 10286, Eugene OR 97440. Phone 1-541/682-6913 or 1-800/452-3670.

PENNSYLVANIA
Covered Bridges of Somerset County, Pennsylvania by Sheldon Barkman, Accurate Printcrafters, Bradenton FL, 1979.

The Covered Bridges of Columbia County, Pennsylvania by Edwin M. Barton, The Columbia County Historical Society, Bloomsburg PA, 1974.

Seeing Lancaster County's Covered Bridges by E. Gipe Caruthers, 1974.

The Colossus of 1812: An American Engineering Superlative by Lee Nelson, ASCE, New York, 1990.

Historic Bridges of Pennsylvania by William Shank, American Canal & Transportation Center, York PA, second edition, 1974.

(Continued on next page)

(Continued from previous page)

Covered Bridges of Pennsylvania Dutchland by Elmer Smith, Applied Arts, Witmer PA, fifth printing, 1966; 19th printing, 1991.

Tracking the Crossings of the Yellow Breeches Creek, Cumberland County, Pennsylvania by Evelyn Thomas, Rea-Craft Press Inc., Foxboro MA, 1981.

The Covered Bridges of Pennsylvania by Susan Zacher, Pennsylvania Historical and Museum Commission, Harrisburg PA, 1982.

Covered Bridges of WBYO Land by Dave Hendricks, Wavelength-Boyertown PA, spring 1975.

The Amazing Pennsylvania Canals by William Shank, American Canal & Transportation Center, York PA, 1975.

Pennsylvania Transportation History by William Shank, American Canal & Transportation Center, York PA, 1990.

Covered Bridges of Pennsylvania by Vera Wagner, Commonwealth of Pennsylvania Internal Affairs, September 1965.

Dedication Souvenir Booklet of the Covered Bridge at Perkasie, Bucks Co., Perkasie Historical Society, 1959.

Dedication Bicentennial Covered Bridge, Sprink Creek Park, College Township, Centre County, 1976.

Perry County Tourist and Recreation Guide, Perry County Tourist Bureau, 1976.

Covered Bridges of Columbia and Montour Counties, map guide by Richard Donovan.

Pennsylvania's Covered Bridges: A Complete Guide by Benjamin and June Evans.

VERMONT

The Covered Bridge by Herbert Wheaton Congdon, Vermont Books, Middlebury VT, third edition, 1959; fifth edition, 1989.

Windham County's Famous Covered Bridges by Victor Morse, The Book Cellar, Brattleboro VT, 1960.

Covered Bridges of Vermont by Ed Barna, The Countryman Press, Woodstock VT 1996.

Covered Wooden Bridges of Bennington County by John Spargo, Bennington Historical Museum and Art Gallery, Bennington VT, 1953.

Vermont's Covered Bridges by Neal Templeton, First Vermont Bank, third edition, 1980.

Sentinels of Time—Vermont's Covered Bridges by Phil Ziegler, Down East Books, Camden ME, 1983.

Spanning Time: Vermont's Covered Bridges by Joseph Nelson.

WEST VIRGINIA
West Virginia's Covered Bridges: A Pictorial Heritage by Stan Cohen.

CANADA
Covered Bridges in the Province de Quebec, Department of Tourism, Fish and Game, circa 1964.

New Brunswick's Covered Bridges by Helen Coldrick, Salisbury, New Brunswick.

No Faster Than a Walk by Stephen and John Gillis, Quispamsis, New Brunswick.

Covered Bridges of Central and Eastern Canada, by Lyn and Richard Harrington, McGraw-Hill Ryerson Limited, Toronto, 1976.

Books and Guides—General

World Guide to Covered Bridges, National Society for the Preservation of Bridges, edited by Richard Donovan, continually updated by Joseph Cohen. Send request with $8 to Irene Eberhardt, 37 Lilac Cir., Marlboro MA 01752.

Romantic Shelters, National Society for the Preservation of Bridges. Send request with $6 to Irene Eberhardt, 37 Lilac Cir., Marlboro MA 01752.

Covered Bridges of the Middle Atlantic States by Richard Sanders Allen, The Stephen Greene Press, Brattleboro VT.

Covered Bridges of the Middle West by Richard Sanders Allen, The Stephen Greene Press, Brattleboro VT, 1970.

Covered Bridges of the Northeast by Richard Sanders Allen, The Stephen Greene Press, Brattleboro VT, 1957. Revised edition, 1983.

Covered Bridges of the South by Richard Sanders Allen, Bonanza Books, New York, 1970.

Old North Country Bridges by Richard Sanders Allen, North Country Books, Utica NY, 1983.

American Covered Bridges—A Pictoral History by Jill Caravan, Courage Books, Philadelphia PA, 1995.

The Last of the Covered Bridge Builders by Milton S. Graton, Clifford-Nicol Inc., Plymouth NH, 1990.

Covered Bridges Today by Brenda Krekeler, Daring Publishing Group, Canton OH, 1989.

Historic American Covered Bridges by Brian McKee, ASCE Press, New York, 1997.

American Barns and Covered Bridges by Eric Sloane, Wilfred Funk Inc., New York, 1954.

Old Covered Bridges by Adelbert Jakeman, Stephen Daye Press, Brattleboro VT, 1935.

Covered Bridges by Herbert Lanks, Covered Bridge Heritage, Jenkintown PA, 1968.

Kissing Bridges by Hegen Peterson, The Stephen Greene Press, Brattleboro VT, 1965.

Historic Highway Bridges in Pennyslvania, Pennsylvania Historical and Museum Commission, 1986.

Covered Bridge Ghost Stories by Karen Zweifel, Crane Hill Publishers, 2923 Crescent Ave., Birmingham AL 35209; 1995.

Internet Addresses

http://www.atawalk.com/united_states.html
(lists all the covered bridges in the U.S. and all the organizations that help save covered bridges)

http://www.brandywinevalley.com
(home page of Chester County, Pennsylvania Tourist Bureau)

http://www.brandywinevalley.com/briddirt/html
(historic covered bridges of Chester County, Pennsylvania)

http://www.co.lane.or.us
(information on bridges in Lane County, Oregon)

http://www.viser.net/~draft/bridges/guide.html
(Oregon covered bridge guide)

http://www.vtonly.com/bridges.html
(Vermont covered bridges)

http://william-king.drexel.edu/top/bridge/CBResources.html
(resources for the study of covered bridges)

http://william-king.www.drexel.edu/top/bridges/cb1.html
(old covered bridges of southeastern Pennsylvania and nearby areas)

http://william-king.www.drexel.edu/top/bridge/ore.html
(selected Oregon covered bridges)

http://william-king.www.drexel.edu/top/bridge/CBOR.HTML
(covered bridges in other regions)

Location Location Location

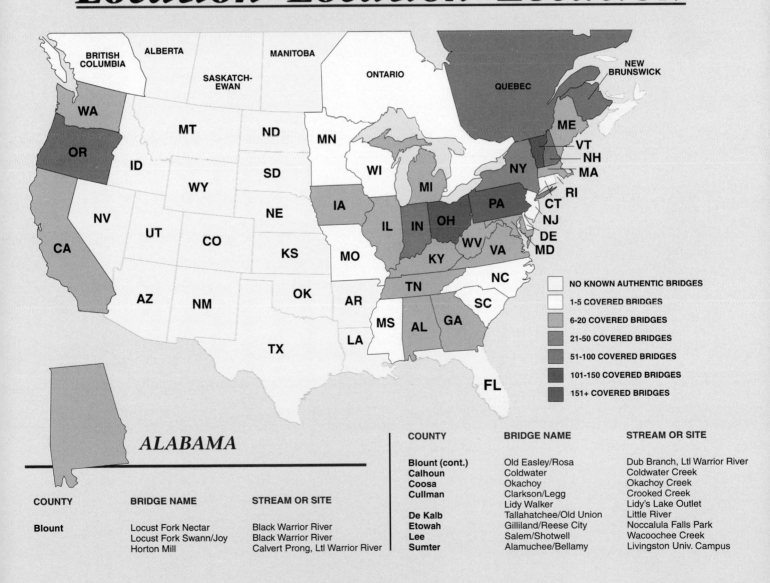

Map Legend:
- NO KNOWN AUTHENTIC BRIDGES
- 1-5 COVERED BRIDGES
- 6-20 COVERED BRIDGES
- 21-50 COVERED BRIDGES
- 51-100 COVERED BRIDGES
- 101-150 COVERED BRIDGES
- 151+ COVERED BRIDGES

ALABAMA

COUNTY	BRIDGE NAME	STREAM OR SITE
Blount	Locust Fork Nectar	Black Warrior River
	Locust Fork Swann/Joy	Black Warrior River
	Horton Mill	Calvert Prong, Ltl Warrior River

COUNTY	BRIDGE NAME	STREAM OR SITE
Blount (cont.)	Old Easley/Rosa	Dub Branch, Ltl Warrior River
Calhoun	Coldwater	Coldwater Creek
Coosa	Okachoy	Okachoy Creek
Cullman	Clarkson/Legg	Crooked Creek
	Lidy Walker	Lidy's Lake Outlet
De Kalb	Tallahatchee/Old Union	Little River
Etowah	Gilliland/Reese City	Noccalula Falls Park
Lee	Salem/Shotwell	Wacoochee Creek
Sumter	Alamuchee/Bellamy	Livingston Univ. Campus

(Continued on next page)

COUNTY	BRIDGE NAME	STREAM OR SITE
Talladega	Kymulga	Talladega Creek
	Waldo/Riddle Mill	Talladega Creek

CALIFORNIA

COUNTY	BRIDGE NAME	STREAM OR SITE
Butte	Honey Run	Butte Creek
	Castleberry	Oregon Creek
Humboldt	Berta's Ranch	Elk River
	Zane's Ranch	Elk River
	Brookwood	Jacoby Creek
Mariposa	Wawona	South Fork, Merced River
Nevada	Bridgeport (private)	South Fork, Yuba River
Santa Cruz	Glen Canyon	Branciforte Creek
	Felton	San Lorenzo River
	Paradise Park	San Lorenzo River
	Roaring Camp	Roaring Creek
Stanislaus	Knights Ferry	Stanislaus River
Yuba	Freeman's Crossing	Oregon Creek

CONNECTICUT

COUNTY	BRIDGE NAME	STREAM OR SITE
Hartford	Huckleberry Hill	Countryside Park
Litchfield	Bull	Housatonic River
	West Cornwall/Hart	Housatonic River
Middlesex	Comstock	Salmon River
	Johnsonville	Moodus River

DELAWARE

COUNTY	BRIDGE NAME	STREAM OR SITE
New Castle	Ashland	Red Clay Creek
	Wooddale (private)	Red Clay Creek

GEORGIA

COUNTY	BRIDGE NAME	STREAM OR SITE
Banks	Lula/Blind	Grove Creek
Barrow-Walton	Kilgore Mill	Apalachee River
Bartow	Lowry	Euharlee Creek
Cobb	Concord/Ruff Mill	Nickajack Creek
De Kalb	College Ave./Stone Mtn.	Stone Mountain Lake
Early	Coheelee Creek	Coheelee Creek
Emanuel	Parrish Mill	Fifteen Mile Creek
Forsythe	Poole Mill	Settingdown Creek
	Burnt/Mashburn Estate	Cumming (private land)
Franklin	Cromer Mill	Nails Creek
Harris	Wehadkee Creek	Calloway Gardens (dry land)
Madison-Oglethorpe	Watson Mill/Carlton	South Fork, Broad River
Meriwether	Big Red Oak Creek	Big Red Oak Creek
Oconee	Elder Mill/Rose Creek	Rose Creek
Oglethorpe	Big Clouds Creek/Howard	Big Clouds Creek
Upson	Hootenville/Auchumpkee	Auchumpkee Creek
White	Stovall Mill/Helen	Chickamauga Creek

COUNTY	BRIDGE NAME	STREAM OR SITE

ILLINOIS

COUNTY	BRIDGE NAME	STREAM OR SITE
Boone	Rockford Bolt Co./Young	Kinnikinnick Creek
Bureau	Red	Big Bureau Creek
DuPage	Centennial	West Branch, DuPage River
	Riverwalk	West Branch, DuPage River
Henderson	Allaman/Eames	Henderson Creek
Knox	Wolf	Spoon River
Randolph	Little Marys	Little Marys River
Sangamon	Glenarm/Hedley	Sugar Creek
Shelby	Thompson Mill	Kaskaskia River

INDIANA

COUNTY	BRIDGE NAME	STREAM OR SITE
Adams	Ceylon	Old Channel, Wabash River
Bartholomew	Brownsville	Mill Run Creek
Brown	Bean Blossom	Bean Blossom Creek
	Ramp Creek	Salt Creek, Brown Co. State Park
Carroll	Adams Mill	Wildcat Creek
	Lancaster/Beard	Wildcat Creek
Dearborn	Guilford	Roadside park, Guilford
Decatur	Westport	Sand Creek
De Kalb	Coburn	St. Joseph River
Fayette	Longwood	Roberts Park (dry land)
Fountain	Wallace	Sugar Mill Creek
	Cade Mill	Coal Creek
	Rob Roy	Big Shawnee Creek
Franklin	Stockheughter	Salt Creek
	Snow Hill	Johnson Fork, Whitewater Riv.
	Seal/Barn	Big Cedar Creek
	Canal Aqueduct	Duck Creek
Gibson	Old Road	Big Bayou Creek
	Wheeling	Patoka River
Grant	Cumberland/Matthews	Mississinewa River
Greene	Richland Creek	Richland Creek
Hamilton	Potter	West Fork, White River
Howard	Vermont	Kockomo Creek
Jackson	Shieldstown	East Fork, White River
	Bell's Ford	East Fork, White River
	Medora	East Fork, White River
Jennings	Scipio	Sand Creek
	James	Big Graham Creek
Lake	Milroy/Crown Point	County Fairgrounds (dry land)
Lawrence	Williams	East Fork, White River
Montgomery	Darlington	Sugar Creek
	Deer Mill	Sugar Creek, Shades State Park
Owen	Cataract Falls	Mill Creek
Parke	Big Rocky Fork	Big Rocky Fork Creek
	Conley's Ford	Big Raccoon Creek
	Jeffries Ford	Big Raccoon Creek
	Bridgeton	Big Raccoon Creek
	Nevins	Little Raccoon Creek
	Thorpe Ford	Big Raccoon Creek
	Roseville	Big Raccoon Creek
	Harry Evans	Rock Run
	Zacke Cox	Rock Run
	Phillips	Big Pond Creek
	Mecca	Big Raccoon Creek
	Sim Smith	Leatherwood Creek
	Catlin	Bill Diddle Creek
	McAllister	Little Raccoon Creek
	Crooks	Williams Creek
	Billie Creek	Williams Creek
	Mansfield	Big Raccoon Creek
	Portland Mills/Dooley Station	Little Raccoon Creek
	Beeson	Billie Creek Village (dry land)
	Leatherwood Station	Williams Creek, Billie Creek Vill.

COUNTY	BRIDGE NAME	STREAM OR SITE
Parke (cont.)	Melcher	Leatherwood Creek
	West Union	Sugar Creek
	Jackson	Sugar Creek
	Mill Creek/Tow Path	Mill Creek
	Coal Creek/Lodi	Coal Creek
	Rush Creek	Rush Creek
	Marshall	Rush Creek
	Bowsher Ford	Mill Creek
	Cox Ford	Sugar Creek
	Wilkins Mill	Sugar Mill
	Narrows	Sugar Creek
Perry-Spencer	Huffman Mill	Anderson River
Putnam	Cornstalk	Cornstalk Creek
	Hillis/Baker Camp	Big Walnut Creek
	Pine Bluff	Big Walnut Creek
	Rollingstone	Big Walnut Creek
	Edna Collins	Little Walnut Creek
	Dunbar	Big Walnut Creek
	Oakalla/Shoppell	Big Walnut Creek
	Houck	Big Walnut Creek
	Dick Huffman	Big Walnut Creek
Ripley	Holton	Otter Creek
	Busching	Laughery Creek
Rush	Smith	Big Flat Rock River
	Offutt's Ford	Little Blue River
	Forsythe Mill	Big Flat Rock River
	Moscow	Big Flat Rock River
	Norris Ford	Big Flat Rock River
	Homer/Barn	Walker Twp. (private land)
Shelby	Cedar Ford	County Fairgrounds (dry land)
Vermillion	South Hill	Brouillett's Creek
	Hillsdale	Ernie Pyle Park (dry land)
	Newport	Little Vermillion River
	Eugene	Vermillion River
Vigo	Irishman	Fowler Park
Wabash	Roann	Eel River
	North Manchester	North Eel River

IOWA

COUNTY	BRIDGE NAME	STREAM OR SITE
Cerro Gordo	Wilkinson Pioneer Park	Branch of Shell Rock River
Keokuk	Delta	North Skunk River
Madison	Cutler/Donahue	Winterset City Park
	Cedar/Casper	Cedar Creek
	Hogback	North River
	Holliwell	Middle River
	Imes/King	Imes Bridge Park
	Roseman/Oak Grove	Middle River
Marion	Hammond	North Cedar
	Marysville/Game Preserve	Wilcox Game Preserve
	Marysville	Marion County Park
Polk	Owens	Yeader Creek County Park

KENTUCKY

COUNTY	BRIDGE NAME	STREAM OR SITE
Bourbon	Colville Pike	Hinkston Creek
Bracken	Walcott/White	Locust Creek
Fleming	Ringo Mill	Fox Creek
	Grange City/Hillsboro	Fox Creek
	Goddard/White	Sandlick Creek
Franklin	Switzer	North Elkhorn Creek
Greenup	Bennett Mill	Tygart's Creek
	Oldtown	Little Sandy Creek
Lewis	Cabin Creek/	
	Mackey-Hughes Farm	Cabin Creek
Mason	Dover	Lee's Creek
	Valley Pike/Bouldin (private)	Lee's Creek Tributary
Robertson	Johnson Creek	Johnson Creek
Washington	Beech Fork/Mooresville	Beech Fork River

COUNTY	BRIDGE NAME	STREAM OR SITE

MAINE

Aroostook	Watson Settlement	Meduxnekeag River
Cumberland	Babb	Presumpscot River
	Lovejoy	Ellis River
	Hemlock	Old Channel, Saco River
	Bennett	Magalloway River
	Sunday River/Artist	Sunday River
Oxford-York	Porter/Parsonfield	Ossippee River
Penobscot	Robyville	Kenduskeag Stream
Piscataquis	Low	Piscataquis River
Somerset	Wire	Carrabassett River
York	Old Route 4	Boston & Maine RR
	Sinnot Road	Boston & Maine RR

MARYLAND

Baltimore-Harford	Jericho Falls	Little Gunpowder River
Cecil	Gilpin	Northeast Creek
	Foxcatcher Farm	DuPont Estate (private land)
Frederick	Utica Mills	Fishing Creek
	Roddy	Owens Creek
	Loys	Owens Creek

MASSACHUSETTS

Berkshire	Upper Sheffield	Housatonic River
Essex	Kent Island	Boston & Maine RR
Franklin	Burkeville	South River
	Pumping Station	Green River
	Arthur Smith	North River
	Bissell	Mill Brook
	Creamery Brook	Creamery Brook (private land)
Hamden	Goodrich	Stanley Park
Hampshire-Worcester	Gilbertville	Ware River
Middlesex	Chester H. Waterous	Nashua River
	Clark Street	Boston & Maine RR
Worcester	Vermont	Old Sturbridge Village
	Service	Old Sturbridge Village
	W. Boylston/Hartwell St.	Boston & Maine RR

MICHIGAN

Ionia	White	Flat River
Kent	Ada/Bradfield	Thornapple River
	Fallasburg	Flat River
Saginaw	Zehnder	Cass River
St. Joseph	Langley	St. Joseph River
Wayne	Ackley	Greenfield Village

MINNESOTA

Goodhue	Zumbrota	Zumbro River

(Continued on next page)

COUNTY	BRIDGE NAME	STREAM OR SITE

MISSISSIPPI

COUNTY	BRIDGE NAME	STREAM OR SITE
Lincoln	May	Boquechitto Creek

MISSOURI

COUNTY	BRIDGE NAME	STREAM OR SITE
Cape Girardeau	Bollinger Mill	Whitewater River
Jefferson	Sandy Creek	Sandy Creek/LeMay Ferry Rd.
Laclede	E.D. Rush	Dry Glaze Creek (private land)
Linn	Locust Creek	Dry Channel/Locust Creek
Monroe	Union	Elk Fork, Salt River

NEW HAMPSHIRE

COUNTY	BRIDGE NAME	STREAM OR SITE
Carroll	Honeymoon	Ellis River
	Bartlett	Saco River
	Saco River	Saco RIver
	Swift River	Swift River
	Albany	Swift River
	Durgin	Cold River
	Whittier	Bearcamp River
Cheshire	Upper Village	Ashuelot River
	Coombs	Ashuelot River
	Thompson/W. Swanzey	Ashuelot River
	Cresson/Sawyers	Ashuelot River
	Slate	Ashuelot River
	Carlton	South Branch, Ashuelot River
Coos	Happy Corner	Perry Stream
	River Road	Perry Stream
	Clarksville/Pittsburg	Connecticut River
	Groveton	Upper Ammonoosuc River
	Stark	Upper Ammonoosuc River
	Mechanic Street	Israel River
	Columbia	Connecticut River
	Mount Orne	Connecticut River
Grafton	Swiftwater	Wild Ammonoosuc River
	Bath	Ammonoosuc River
	Bath-Haverhill/Woodsville	Ammonoosuc River
	Flume	Pemigewasset River
	Turkey Jim	West Branch Brook
	Bump	Beebe River
	Blair	Pemigewasset River
	Smith	Baker River
	Edgell	Clay Brook
	Clark/Pinsley	Pemigewasset River
	Brundage	Mill Brook (private land)
	Jack O'Lantern Resort	Keating Country Club
Hillsborough	County	Contoocook River
	Russell Hill Road	Wilton Blood Brook
Merrimack	Cilleyville	Blackwater River
	Keniston	Blackwater River
	Bement	West Branch, Warner River
	Waterloo	Warner River
	Dalton	Warner River
	Contoocook Railroad	Contoocook River
	Rowell	Contoocook River
	Sulphite Railroad	Winnipesaukee River
	New England College	On campus (private)
Stratford	Rollinsford	Boston & Maine RR
Sullivan	Blacksmith Shop	Cornish Mill Brook
	Dingleton	Cornish Mill Brook

COUNTY	BRIDGE NAME	STREAM OR SITE
Sullivan (cont.)	Pier Railroad	Sugar River
	Wright Railroad	Sugar River
	Corbin	Croydon Branch, Sugar River
	McDermott	Cold River
	Drewsville/Prentiss	Great Brook
	Meriden/Mill	Bloods Brook
	Bayliss/Bridge Over Gorge	Blow-Me-Down Brook
	Cornish-Windsor	Connecticut River

NEW JERSEY

COUNTY	BRIDGE NAME	STREAM OR SITE
Hunterdon	Green Sergeants	Wickeheoke Creek

NEW YORK

COUNTY	BRIDGE NAME	STREAM OR SITE
Albany	Waldbillig	Vly Creek (private road)
Delaware	Downsville	East Branch, Delaware River
	Fitches	West Branch, Delaware River
	Hamden	West Branch, Delaware River
	Tuscarora Club/Demis	Mill Brook (private road)
	Campbell	Trout Brook (private land)
	Erpf	Arkville Brook (private land)
Essex	Jay	East Brook, Ausable River
Fulton	Eagle Mills	Kenyetto Creek
Herkimer	Salisbury Center	Spruce Creek
Jefferson	Frontenac/North Country	Belleville (private land)
Madison	Americana Village	Mill Pond (private land)
Ostego	Hyde Hall	Shadow Brook/ Glimmerglass State Park
Rensselaer	Buskirk	Hoosic River
Saratoga	Copeland	Beecher Creek
Schoharie	Blenheim	Schoharie Creek
Sullivan	Halls Mills	Neversink River
	Beaverkill/Conklin	Beaverkill Creek
	Van Tran Flat/Livingston Manor	Willowemoc Creek
	Bendo	Willowemoc Creek
Tompkins	Newfield	West Branch, Cayuga Creek
Ulster	Perrine	Wallkill River
	Forge	Dry brook on private road
	Tappan/Kittle	Dry brook on Erickson Road
	Olive/Turnwood	Old Channel, Esopus Creek
	Grants Mills	Mill Brook
Washington	Eagleville	Batten Kill
	Shushan (private museum)	Batten Kill
	Rexleigh	Batten Kill

NORTH CAROLINA

COUNTY	BRIDGE NAME	STREAM OR SITE
Bertie	Rascoe Mills	Conniott Creek
	Hoggard Gristmill	Hoggard Mill Creek
	Hoggard Sawmill	Hoggard Mill Creek
Catawba	Bunker Hill	Lyle Creek
Randolph	Pisgah	Upper Branch, Little River

COUNTY	BRIDGE NAME	STREAM OR SITE

OHIO

COUNTY	BRIDGE NAME	STREAM OR SITE
Adams	Harshaville	Cherry Fork, Ohio Brush Creek
	Kirker	East Fork, Eagle Creek
Ashtabula	Olin/Dewey Road	Ashtabula River
	Creek Road	Conneaut Creek
	Middle Road	Conneaut Creek
	Root Road	West Branch, Ashtabula River
	Benetka Road	Ashtabula River
	Graham Road	Graham Road (dry land)
	South Denmark Road	Mill Creek
	Muller/Doyle Road	Mill Creek
	Mechanicsville	Grand River
	Harpersfield	Grand River
	Riverdale Road	Grand River
	Warner Hollow	Phelps Creek
	State Road	Conneaut Creek
	Caine Road	West Branch, Ashtabula River
Athens	Palos	Sunday Creek
	Kidwell	Sunday Creek
	Blackwood	Middle Branch, Shade River
Auglaize	Wellman	Muddy Creek (private road)
Belmont	Shaeffer/Campbell	Belmont University Campus
Brown	Brown	White Oak Creek
	New Hope/Bethel Road	White Oak Creek
	McCafferty	East Fork, Little Miami River
	Bowman/Eagle	Eagle Creek
	Scofield/Martin Hill	Beetle Creek
	Pole Road	Huntington Twp.
	George Miller	West Fork, Eagle Creek
Butler	State Line/Bebb Park	Dry Fork Creek
	Black/Pughs Mill	Four Mile Creek
Clermont	Perintown/Stonelick	Stonelick Creek
Clinton-Highland	Martinsville Road	Todds Fork, Little Miami River
	Lynchburg	East Fork, Little Miami River
Columbiana	Sells/Roller Mill	West Fork, Little Beaver Creek
	McClellan/Kinmuer	West Fork, Little Beaver Creek
	Teegarden/Centennial	Middle Fork, Little Beaver Creek
	Lisbon/Miller Road	Mill Site Creek
	Thomas J. Malone	Gaston Mill, Beaver Creek Park
Coshocton	Helmick	Killbuck Creek
	Hamilton Farm	Wills Creek
Delaware	Chambers Road	Big Walnut Creek
Fairfield	Hizey/Visintine	Sycamore Creek
	Jon Bright No. 2	Lancaster campus, Ohio Univ.
	George Hutchins	Clear Creek
	Hannaway	Clear Creek
	Johnson	Clear Creek
	Zeller-Smith	Sycamore
	Shade	Pierson Farm (dry land)
	McLeery	James Walters property
	Shryer	Bill Shryer Farm
	Charles Holliday	Corn Festival grounds (dry land)
	R.F. Baker	Fairfield Union H.S.
	Jon Raab	Ireland Road (dry land)
	Hartman No. 2	Ohio & Erie Canalbed
	Mae Hummel	Rush Creek
	Mink Hollow	Arney Run
	Rock Mill	Hocking River
	Roley Schoolhouse	County fairgrounds (dry land)
	Jackson/Ety	Walnut Creek
Franklin	Bergstresser	Walnut Creek
	Brannon/Wesner	Big Run (private land)
Greene	Cemetery Road	Yellow Springs Creek
	West Engle Mill Road	Anderson Fork, Caesar Creek
	Stevenson Road	Massies Creek
	Charleton Mill	Massies Creek
	Ballard Road	North Branch, Caesar Creek
Guernsey	Indian Camp	Indian Camp Run
	Armstrong/Clio	Cambridge City Park
	Reservoir	Leatherwood Creek
Hamilton	Jediah Hill/Groff Mill	West Fork, Mill Creek
Harrison	Skull Fork	Skull Fork, Stillwater Creek
Jackson	Petersburg/Johnson Rd.	Little Scioto River
	Byer	Pigeon Creek
	Buckeye Furnace	Little Raccoon Creek
Lawrence	Scottown/Pleasant Ridge	Indian Guyan Creek

COUNTY	BRIDGE NAME	STREAM OR SITE
Licking	Belle Hall	Otter Fork, Licking River
	Boy Scout Camp (private)	Rocky Fork Creek
	Mercer/Girl Scout Camp	Wakatomika Creek
	Gregg	Wakatomika Creek
	Lobdell Park	Firemans Park (dry land)
	Davis Farm	Rocky Fork, Licking River
	Maple Run	Bennington Twp. Fairgrounds (dry land)
Logan	McColly	Great Miami River
	Bickham	South Fork, Great Miami River
Miami	Eldean	Great Miami River
Monroe	Foraker	Little Muskingum River
	Long/Knowlton	Little Muskingum River
Montgomery	Germantown	Little Twin Creek
	Feedwire Road	Miami & Erie Canalbed
	Jasper Road	Mud Lick Creek
Morgan	Barkhurst Mill (private)	Wolf Creek
	Rosseau	McConnellsville County Fairgrounds (dry land)
	Helmick Mill	Island Run
	Adams/San Toy	San Toy Creek
	Milton Dye	Brannons Fork, Mill Creek
Muskingum	Johnson Mill/Salt Creek	Salt Creek
Noble	Manchester	Olive Green Creek
	Parrish	Sharon Fork, Olive Green Creek
	Guerst/Otter Slide	County Fairgrounds
	Danford	Keith Fork, Olive Green Creek
	Huffman Wood	Middle Fork, Duck Creek
Perry	Parks/South	Painter Creek
	Hopewell Church	Painter Creek
	Jacks Hollow	Kents Run
	Bowman Mill/Redington (private)	County Fairgrounds (dry land)
	Mary Ruffner (private)	Somerset Road
Pickaway	Valentine	Bill Green Farm
Preble	Harshman	Four Mile Creek
	Dixon Branch	Civitan Park (dry land)
	Roberts	Seven Mile Creek
	Brubaker	Sams Run
	Christman	Seven Mile Creek
	Geeting	Price Creek
	Warnke	Swamp Creek
Ross	Buckskin	Buckskin Creek
Sandusky	Mull	East Branch, Wolf Creek
Scioto	Bennett Schoolhouse/Harrison Hill	Little Scioto River
	Otway	Scioto Brush Creek
Shelby	Lockington	West Channel, Great Miami River
Summit	Everett Road	Furnace Run
Trumbull	Newton Falls	East Branch, Mahoning River
Union	Upper Darby/Pottersburg	Big Darby Creek
	Spain Creek	Spain Creek
	Winget Road/Treacle Creek	Treacle Creek
	Bigelow/Little Darby	Little Darby Creek
	Reed/London Road	Big Darby Creek
Vinton	Mt. Olive/Grand Staff	Middle Fork, Salt Creek
	Bay/Tinker	Junior Fairgrounds
	Geer Mill/Humpback	Raccoon Creek
	Easkin Mill/Arbaugh	Raccoon Creek
	Cox	Brushy Fork, Raccoon Creek
Washington	Shinn	West Branch, Wolf Creek
	Henry	West Branch, Little Hocking River
	Root	South Branch Wolf Creek
	Harra	South Branch Wolf Creek
	Bell	Southwest Fork/Wolf Creek
	Mill Branch	Barlow Fairgrounds
	Schwenderman	Jackson Hill Park (dry land)
	Hills/Hildreth	Little Muskingum River
	Hune	Little Muskingum River
	Rinard	Little Muskingum River
Wyandot	Parker	Sandusky River
	Swartz	Sandusky River

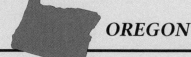

OREGON

COUNTY	BRIDGE NAME	STREAM OR SITE
Benton	Harris	Marys River
	Hayden	Alsea River
	Irish Bend	Willamette Slough
Coos	Sandy Creek	Sandy Creek

(Continued on next page)

COUNTY	BRIDGE NAME	STREAM OR SITE
Douglas	Krewson/Pass	Pass Creek
	Rochester	Calapooya Creek
	Cavitt Creek	Little River
	Neal Lane	South Fork, Myrtle Creek
	Roaring Camp	Elk Creek (private road)
Jackson	Antelope Creek	Little Butte Creek
	Lost Creek	Lost Creek
	Wimer	Evans Creek
	McKee	Middle Fork, Applegate River
Josephine	Sunny Valley	Grave Creek
Lane	Coyote Creek/Swing Log	Coyote Creek
	Wildcat	Wildcat Creek
	Lake Creek/Nelson Creek	Lake Creek
	Goodpasture	McKenzie River
	Belknap	McKenzie River
	Horse Creek	Horse Creek
	Pengra	Fall Creek
	Unity	Fall Creek
	Lowell	Middle Fork, Willamette River
	Parvin	Lost Creek
	Dorena/Star	Row River
	Currin	Row River
	Mosby Creek	Mosby Creek
	Stewart	Mosby Creek
	Earnest/Russell	Mohawk River
	Deadwood	Deadwood Creek
	Office (private)	Middle Fork, Willamette River
	Chambers RR	Willamette River (abandoned RR)
	Centennial	Coast Fork, Willamette River
Lincoln	Chitwood	Yaquina River
	North Fork of the Yachats	North Fork, Yachats River
	Fisher School	Five River
	Upper Drift Creek	Upper Drift Creek
Linn	Hannah	Thomas Creek
	Shimanek	Thomas Creek
	Gilkey	Thomas Creek
	Weddle/Devaney	Thomas Creek
	Larwood	Crabtree Creek
	Bohemian Hall/Richardson Gap	Crabtree Creek
	Hoffman	Crabtree Creek
	Short/Cascadia	South Santiam River
	Crawfordsville	Calapooia River
	Dahlenburg/Holley Replica	Ames Creek
Marion	Gallon House	Abiqua Creek
	Jordan Power Canal	Pioneer Park
Polk	Ritner Creek	Ritner Creek
	Alva "Doc" Fourtner	S. Yamhill River (private land)

PENNSYLVANIA

COUNTY	BRIDGE NAME	STREAM OR SITE
Adams	Saucks	Marsh Creek
	Reeser/Anderson Farm	Stoney Point Road (private)
	Jacks Mountain	Toms Creek
	Heike (private)	Bermudian Creek
Bedford	Felton Mill	Brush Creek
	Heirline/Kinton	Raystown
	Claycomb/Reynoldstown	Raystown Branch, Juniata Riv.
	Halls Mill	Yellow Creek
	Kinsley	Dunning Creek (private land)
	Ryot	Dunning Creek
	Cuppet/New Paris	Dunning Creek
	Diehl/Turner	Raystown Branch, Juniata Riv.
	Fichtner/Palo Alto	Gladdens Run
	Bowser/Osterburg	Bobs Creek
	Snooks	Dunning Creek
	Colvin	Shawnee Creek
	Jackson Mill	Brush Creek
	Hewitt	Town Creek
Berks	Pleasantville	Little Manatawny Creek
	Greisemer Mill	Manatawny Creek
	Kutz Mill/Sacony	Sacony Creek
	Wertz/Red	Tulpehocken Creek
	Dreibelbis Station	Maiden Creek
Bradford	Knapp	Browns Creek
Bucks	Knecht/Sleifer	Durham Creek
	Van Sant	Pidcock Creek
	Erwinna	Roaring Rocks Creek
	South Perkasie	Lenape Park (dry land)

COUNTY	BRIDGE NAME	STREAM OR SITE
Bucks (cont.)	Sheard Mill	Tohickon Creek
	Mood	East Branch, PerkiomenCreek
	Uhlerstown	Delaware Canal
	Frankenfield	Tinicum Creek
	Cabin Run	Cabin Run
	Loux	Cabin Run
	Iron Hill/Pine Valley	Pine Run
	Twining Ford/Schofield Ford	Tyler State Park
	Ralph Stover State Park	Tohickon Creek
Carbon	Harrity/Bucks	Beltzville State Park (dry land)
	Little Gap	Princess Creek
Chester	Rudolph & Arthur	Big Elk Creek
	Glen Hope	Little Elk Creek
	Linton Stevens	Big Elk Creek
	Speakman No. 1	Buck Run
	Speakman No. 2/ Mary Ann Pyle	Buck Run (private farm road)
	Hayes Clark	Doe Run
	Gibson/Harmony Hill	East Branch, Brandywine Creek
	Larkin	Branch of Marsh Creek
	Hall/Sheeder	French Creek
	Kennedy	French Creek
	Rapp	French Creek
	Knox/Valley Forge	Valley Creek
Chester-Delaware	Bartram/Goshen	Crum Creek
Chester-Lancaster	Mercer	Octoraro Creek
	Pine Grove	Octoraro Creek
Clearfield	McGees Mills	West Branch, Susquehanna River
Clinton	Logan Mill	Big Fishing Creek
Columbia	Fowlersville	Branch of Briar Creek
	Shoemaker	Branch Run
	Sam Eckman	Little Fishing Creek
	Josiah Hess/Laubach	Huntington Creek
	East Paden	Huntington Creek Overflow
	West Paden	Huntington Creek
	Snyder	Roaring Creek
	Wagner	Roaring Creek
	Davis	Roaring Creek
	Wanich	Little Fishing Creek
	Esther Furnace	Roaring Creek
	Stillwater	Fishing Creek
	Kramer	Mud Run
	Jud Christian	Little Fishing Creek
	Patterson	Green Creek
	Paar Mill	Roaring Creek
	Rohrbach	South Branch, Roaring Creek
	Rupert	Fishing Creek
	Hollingshead	Catawissa Creek
	Creasyville	Little Fishing Creek
	Johnson	Mugser Run
	Krickbaum	South Branch, Roaring Creek
	Lawrence L. Knoebel (priv.)	South Branch, Roaring Creek
	Richards	South Branch, Roaring Creek
	Roaring Creek	Cleveland
Cumberland	Thompson	Conodoquinet Creek
	Ramp	Conodoquinet Creek
	Bowmansdale/Stoner	Yellow Breeches Creek
Dauphin	Wilhour Mill	Wisconisco Creek
	Everhart/Fort Hunter	Fort Hunter Museum (private)
	Henninger Farm/Stroup	Wisconisco Creek
Erie	Sherman/Keepville	West Branch, Conneaut Creek
	Gudgeonville	Elk Creek
	Waterford	LeBoeuf Creek
	Carmen/Perry	Conneaut Creek
Franklin	Martins Mill/Shindle	Conocheague Creek
	Red/Witherspoon	Licking Creek
Greene	Carmichael	Muddy Creek
	Grimes	Ruff Creek
	King	Hoover Run
	Lippincott/Cox Farm	Ruff Creek
	Nettie Wood	Pursley Creek
	Neils/Red	Whiteley Creek
	Scott	South Fork, Tenmile Creek
	Shriver	Hargus Creek
	White	Whiteley Creek
Greene-Washington	Davis/Horn	Tenmile Creek
Huntingdon	St. Mary/Shade Gap	Shade Creek
Indiana	Trusal/Dice Plum Creek	South Branch, Plum Creek
	Harmon	South Branch, Plum Creek
	Kintersburg	Crooked Creek
	Thomas	Crooked Creek
Jefferson	McCracken (private)	Wakefield Springs Farm

COUNTY	BRIDGE NAME	STREAM OR SITE
Juniata	Academia/Pomeroy	Tuscarora Creek
	Dimmsville	Cocolamus Creek
	Lehman/Port Royal (private)	Port Licking Creek
	Oriental/Currys Corner	Mahantango Creek
	Meisers Mill/Shaeffer	Mahantango Creek
Lancaster	Pool Forge (private)	Conestoga River
	Weaver Mill/White Hall	Conestoga River
	Kurtz Mill/Bears Mill	Mill Creek
	Eberly/Bitzers Mill	Conestoga River
	Pinetown	Conestoga River
	Hunsecker Mill	Conestoga River
	Oberholtzers Mill/Red Run	Muddy Creek
	Buchers Mill	Cocalico Creek
	Keller/Rettews Mill	Cocalico Creek
	Rosehill/Wenger	Cocalico Creek
	Hess Mill/Buck Hill Farm	Warwick Twp. (private land)
	Landis Mill	Little Conestoga Creek
	White Rock Forge	West Branch, Octoraro Creek
	Leaman Pl./Eshelman Mill	Pequea Creek
	Herr Mill/Soudersburg (priv.)	Pequea Creek
	Neff Mill	Pequea Creek
	Lime Valley	Pequea Creek
	Baumgardner Mill	Pequea Creek
	Colemanville/Maric Forge	Pequea Creek
	Forry Mill	Big Chikiswalunga Creek
	Shenck Mill	Big Chikiswalunga Creek
	Jacob Shearer (private)	Big Chikiswalunga Creek
	Kauffman/Distillery	Big Chikiswalunga Creek
	Jackson Sawmill	West Branch, Octoraro Creek
	Hammer Creek	Erbs Bridge Road
	Risser Mill	Little Chikiswalunga Creek
	Seigrist Mill/Moore Mill	Big Chikiswalunga Creek
	Willows (private)	Branch of Mill Creek
Lawrence	McConnells Mills	Slippery Rock Creek
	Banks	Neshannock Creek
Lehigh	Bogert	Little Lehigh Creek
	Wehr	Jordan Creek
	Manassas Guth	Jordan Creek
	Rex	Jordan Creek
	Geiger	Jordan Creek
	Schlicher	Jordan Creek
Luzerne	Bittenbender	Huntington Creek
Lycoming	Buttonwood	Blockhouse Creek
	Cogan House/Buckhorn	Larrys Creek
	Fraser/Moreland	Little Muncy Creek
Mercer	Kidds Mill	Shenango River
Montour	Sam Wagner/Gottlieb Brown	Chillisquaque Creek
	Old Keefer	Chillisquaque Creek
Northampton	Solts Mill/Kreidersville	Hokenduqua Creek
Northumberland	Keefer Station	Shamokin Creek
	Rishel	Chillisquaque Creek
	Rebuck/Himmel Church	Schwaben Creek
	Mertz (private)	Mirkwood Road
Perry	Flickinger Mill/Bistline	Shermans Creek
	Cisna Mill/Adair	Shermans Creek
	Red	Wildcat Creek
	Saville	Big Buffalo Creek
	Kochenderfer	Big Buffalo Creek
	Landisburg/Rice	Shermans Creek
	New Germantown	New Shermans Creek
	Mount Pleasant	Shermans Creek
	Book/Kaufman	Shermans Creek
	Enslow/Turkey Tail	Shermans Creek
	Wagoners Mill/Thompson	Bixler Run
	Dellville	Shermans Creek
	Fleisher	Big Buffalo Creek
	Clay/Wahneta	Little Buffalo Creek
Philadelphia	Thomas Mill	Wissahickon Creek
Schuylkill	Zimmerman	Little Swatara Creek
	Rock	Little Swatara Creek
Snyder	Beavertown/Dreese	Middle Creek
	Klinepeter/Overflow	Middle Creek
	Aline/Meiserville	North Branch, Mahantango Creek
Somerset	Burkholder	Buffalo Creek
	Packsaddle/Doc Miler	Brush Creek
	Barronvale (private)	Laurel Hill Creek
	Cox Creek/Roberts	Haupt Museum
	King (private)	Laurel Hill Creek
	Glessner	Stony Creek
	New Baltimore	Juniata River
	Trostletown/Kantner	Stony Creek
	Shaffer/Bens Creek	Bens Creek
	Humbert/Faidley	Laurel Hill Creek

COUNTY	BRIDGE NAME	STREAM OR SITE
Sullivan	Forksville	Loyalsock Creek
	Hillsgrove/Rinkers	Loyalsock Creek
	Davidson/Sonestown	Muncy Creek
Susquehanna	L.C. Beavan/Old Mill Village	New Milford Twp. (private road)
Union	Millmont/Glen Iron	Penns Creek
	Hayes	Buffalo Creek
	Hassenplug	Buffalo Creek
	Factory/Horsham	White Deer Creek
	Gordon Hufnagle Mem. Park	Lewisburg Bull Run
Washington	Sprowl	Rocky Run
	Bailey	Tenmile Creek of Wheeling Creek
	Brownlee/Stout	Templeton Fork, Wheeling Creek
	Crawford	Robinson Fork of Wheeling Creek
	Danley	Robinson Run
	Day	Short Creek
	Devils Den/McClurg	Hanover Twp. Park
	Ebenezer Church	Branch of Mingo Creek
	Erskine	Middle Wheeling Creek
	Henry	Mingo Creek
	Hughes	Tenmile Creek of Wheeling Creek
	Jacksons Mill	Kings Creek
	Krepps	Raccoon Creek
	Leatherman	South Branch, Pigeon Creek
	Lyle	Brush Run
	Longdon/Miller	Templeton Fork of Wheeling Creek
	Blaney/May	Branch of Middle Wheeling Creek
	Plant Wheeling Creek	Templeton Fork
	Freeman/Ralston (private)	Aunt Clara's Fork, King Creek
	Wilsons Mill	Cross Creek
	Wyit Sprowls	Robinson Run
	Wright/Cerl	North Branch, Pigeon Creek
	Sawhill	Buffalo Creek
	Pine Bank/Meadowcroft Vill.	Jefferson Twp. (private land)
Westmoreland	Bells Mills	Sewickley Creek

SOUTH CAROLINA

COUNTY	BRIDGE NAME	STREAM OR SITE
Greenville	Campbell	Beaver Dam

TENNESSEE

COUNTY	BRIDGE NAME	STREAM OR SITE
Carter	Elizabethton	Doe River
Greene	Bible/Chucky	Little Chucky Creek
Hamblen	Clifford Holder	Knox Brook
Montgomery	Port Royal	Port Red River
Obion	Parks Farm (private)	Obion River drainage canal
Sevier	Pigeon	East Fork, Little Pigeon River

VERMONT

COUNTY	BRIDGE NAME	STREAM OR SITE
Addison	Station	Otter Creek
	Hollow/Old Covered Bridge Farm	Ferrisburg (private land)
	Halpin	Muddy Branch, New Haven River
	Pulp Mill	Otter Creek
	East Shoreham RR	Lemon Fair River
Bennington	Bridge at the Green	Batten Kill
	Henry	Walloomsac River
	Papermill Village	Walloomsac River
	Silk/Locust Grove	Walloomsac River
	Chiselville	Roaring Branch, Batten Kill

(Continued on next page)

COUNTY	BRIDGE NAME	STREAM OR SITE
Caledonia	Greenbank Hollow	Joe's Brook
	Schoolhouse/Chase	S. Wheelock Branch, Passumpic River
	Chamberlin/Whitcomb	S. Wheelock Branch, Passumpsic River
	Sanborn	Passumpsic River (priv. land)
	Millers Run	Millers Run
	Randall/Burlington (priv.)	East Branch, Passumpsic River
Chittendon	Lake Shore	Holmes Creek
	Upper/Sequin	Lewis Creek
	Quinlan/Lower	Lewis Creek
	Westford	Browns River
	Cambridge	Burr Pond
Essex	Columbia	Connecticut River
	Mount Orne	Connecticut River
Franklin	Hopkins	Trout River
	Village/Maple Street	Fairfax Mill Brook
	East Fairfield	East Black Creek
	Comstock	Trout River
	Fuller/Black Falls	Black Falls Brook
	Hectorville	South Branch, Trout River
	Hutchins	South Branch, Trout River
	Longley/Harnois	Trout River
	West Hill/Creamery	West Hill Brook
Lamoille	Scott/Gristmill	Brewster River
	Poland/Station	Lamoille River
	Little/Gates Farm (private)	Seymour River
	Mill	North Branch, Lamoille River
	Morgan	North Branch, Lamoille River
	Power House	Gihon River
	Scribner	Gihon River
	Red/Sterling	Sterling Brook
	Stowe Hollow/Gold Brook	Gold Brook
	Village/Church Street	North Branch, Lamoille River
	Montgomery	North Branch, Lamoille River
	Jaynes/Codding Hollow	North Branch, Lamoille River
	Fisher Railroad	Lamoille River
Orange	Moxley/Guy	First Branch, White River
	Kingsbury/Hyde	Second Branch, White River
	Gifford/C.K. Smith	Second Branch, White River
	Blaisdell/Braley	Second Branch, White River
	Union Village	Ompompanoosuc River
	Sayres	Ompompanoosuc River
	Howe	First Branch, White River
	Cilley/Lower	First Branch, White River
	Mill/Hayward & Noble	First Branch, White River
	Larkin	First Branch, White River
	Flint	First Branch, White River
Orleans	Orne	Black River (private land)
	Coventry/Lower	Black River
	River Road/School	Missisquoi River
Rutland	Sanderson	Otter Creek
	Kingsley	Mill River
	Gorham/Goodnough	Otter Creek
	Hammond	Otter Creek
	Depot	Otter Creek
	Cooley	Furnace Brook
	Brown	Cold River
	Twin	Rutland (private land)
Washington	Coburn/Cemetary	Winooski River
	Orton Farm/Martin (private)	Winooski River
	Moseley	Stony Brook
	Station/Northfield Falls	Dog River
	Slaughter House	Dog River
	Lower/Newell	Cox Brook
	Upper	Cox Brook
	Pine Brook	Pine Brook
	Village	Mad River
	Warren	Mad River
	Robbins Nest	Winooski River
Windham	Creamery	Whetstone Brook
	West Dummerston	West River
	Kidder	South Branch, Saxtons River
	Green River	Green River
	Williamsville	Rock River
	Hall	Saxtons River
	Worrall	Williams River
	Bartonsville	Williams River
	Scott	West River
Windsor	Martins Mill	Lulls Brook
	Willard	Ottauquechee River
	Baltimore	Springfield Brook
	Salmond	Sherman Brook
	Upper Falls	Black River
	Best	Mill Brook
	Bowers	Mill Brook
	Taftsville	Ottauquechee River

COUNTY	BRIDGE NAME	STREAM OR SITE
Windsor (cont.)	Lincoln	Ottauquechee River
	Middle/Union	Ottauquechee River
	Twigg-Smith	Mill Brook
	South Pomfret	Barnard Brook
	Cornish-Windsor	Connecticut River

VIRGINIA

COUNTY	BRIDGE NAME	STREAM OR SITE
Alleghany	Humpback	Dunlap Creek roadside park
Campbell	Marysville	Seneca Creek
Giles	Sinking Creek	Newport Sinking Creek
	Link Farm (private)	Sinking Creek
	Red Maple Farm (private)	Sinking Creek
Patrick	Bob White	Smith River
	Jacks Creek	Smith River
Rockingham	Biedler Farm	Smith Creek (private road)
Shenandoah	Meems Bottom	North Fork, Shenandoah River

WASHINGTON

COUNTY	BRIDGE NAME	STREAM OR SITE
Clark	Milbrandt (private)	Salmon Creek
Grays Harbor	Schafer Farm (private)	Carl Schafer Farm Estates
Lewis	PeEll	Chehalis River
Wahkiakum	Grays River	Grays River
Whatcom	Sudden Valley	Little Strawberry Creek
Whitman	Colfax Road	Palouse River

WEST VIRGINIA

COUNTY	BRIDGE NAME	STREAM OR SITE
Barbour	Philippi	Tygart Valley River
	Carrollton	Buckhannon River
Cabell	Milton/Sinks Mill	Milton Mud River
Doddridge	Center Point	Pike Fork, McElroy Creek
Greenbrier	Herns Mill	Milligan Creek
	Hokes Mill	Second Creek
Harrison	Fletcher	Ten Mile Creek
	Simpson Creek/Hollen Mill	Simpson Creek
Jackson	Sarvis Fork	Left Fork, Sandy Creek
	Staats Mill	Cedar Lakes Camp
Lewis	Old Red/Walkersville	Right Fork, West Fork River
Marion	Barrackville	Buffalo Creek
Monongalia	Dents Run/Laurel Point	Dents Run
Monroe	Laurel Creek/Lillydale	Laurel Creek
	Indian Creek/Salt Sulphur Springs	Indian Creek
Pocahontas	Denmar/Locust Creek	Locust Creek
Wetzel	Hundred/Fish Creek	Hundred Fish Creek

WISCONSIN

COUNTY	BRIDGE NAME	STREAM OR SITE
Grant	Stonefield Village	Dewey Creek
Ozaukee	Cedarburg	Cedar Creek

CANADA

	BRIDGE NAME	STREAM OR SITE
BRITISH COLUMBIA		
Similkameen Div.	Ashnola River Rd.	Similkameen River
NEW BRUNSWICK		
Albert	Bamford/Colpitts	Coverdale River
	Crooked Creek	Crooked Creek
	Lower Forty-Five	Forty Five River
	Point Wolfe	Point Wolfe River
	Peter Jonah	Turtle Creek

COUNTY	BRIDGE NAME	STREAM OR SITE
Albert (cont.)	Germantown Lake	Shepody River
	Hartley Steeves	Weldon Creek
	Sawmill Creek	Sawmill Creek
Carleton	Adair	N. Branch, Becaguimec River
	Ellis	N. Branch, Becaguimec River
	Florenceville	St. John River
	Hartland	St. John River
	Keenan/Monquart	Monquart River
	Lockhart Mill	Shiktehawk River
	Mangrum	Becaguimec River
	Benton	Eel River
Charlotte	Canal	Canal Stream
	Dumbarton	Digdeguash River
	Flume Ridge	Magaguadavic River
	Maxwell Crossing	Dennis Stream
	Mcguire	Digdeguash River
	Mill Pond	Little Lepreau River
	McCann	Digdeguash River
	Stillwater	Digdeguash River
Kent	Tom Graham	Tom Graham Creek
	St. Nicholas River	St. Nicholas River
	Camerons Mill	Kouchibouguasis River
Kings	Bloomfield	Bloomfield Creek
	Centreville	Mill Stream River
	Darlings Island	Hammond River
	French Village	Hammond River
	Malone	Kennebecasis River
	Marven	Belleisle Creek
	Macfarlane	Wards Creek
	Bayswater	Milkish Inlet
	Moores Mills	Trout Creek
	Oldfield	Smith Creek
	Plumwesweep	Kennebecasis River
	Urney	Trout Creek
	Salmon	Kennebecasis River
	Smithtown	Hammond River
	Tranton	Smith Creek
	Bell	Trout Creek
	Moosehorn	Moosehorn Brook
Madawaska	Boniface	Green River
	Iroquois River	Iroquois River
	Morneault	Baker Brook
	Quisibis	Quisibis River
Northumberland	Nelson Hollow (private)	Mill Brook
Queens	Burpee	Gaspereau River
	Aaron Clark	Canaan River
	Starkey	Long Creek
	Bayard	Nerepis River
St. John	Tynemouth	Tynemouth Creek
	Irish River	Vaughan Creek
	Hardscrabble Hill	Vaughan Creek
Sunbury	Bell/South Oromocto	S. Branch, Oromocto River
	Hoyt Station	Back Creek
	Mill Settlement	S. Branch, Oromocto River
	Patrick Owen	Rusagonis River
Victoria	Tomilson Mill	Odellach River
Westmoreland	Budd	Cocagne River
	Joshua Gallant	Shediac River
	Boudreau	Memramcook River
	Hasty	Petitcodiac River
	Poirier	Cocagne Rivr
	Wheaton	Tantramar River
	Parkindale	Magnetic Hill Game Park
York	Nackawick Siding	Nackawick Stream
	Stone Ridge	Keswick River
ONTARIO		
Waterloo	Kissing	Grand River
QUEBEC		
Abitibi-Est	Alphonse Normardin	Davy River
	Turgeon	Villemontel River
	St. Maurice	Harricana River
	Carrier	Senneville River
	Champagne	Vassan River
Abitibi-Ouest	Calamite	Desmeloizes River
	Bouchard	Bouchard Creek
	de Chazel	La Sarre River
	Molesworth	Lois River
	du Petit Quatre	Desmeloizes River
	Rang II	Villemontel River
	des Souvenirs	Turgeon River
	Turgeon	Turgeon River
	Levasseur	Macamic River
	Paradis	Turgeon River
	Chazel	Deception Creek

COUNTY	BRIDGE NAME	STREAM OR SITE
Arthabaska	Perreault/Charbonneau	Des Pins River
Beauce	Perreault	Chaudiere River
	Bolduc	Dupuis River
	Napoleon Grondin	St. Victor River
Berthier	Grandchamp	Bayonne River
Bonaventure	du Club	Port Danielk Nord River
	St. Edgar	Petite Cascapedia River
Brome	Balthazard	Yamaska River
	Decelles	Yamaska River
	Province Hill	Mud Creek
Champlain	Bordeleau	Des Envies River
Charlevoix	St. Placide (private)	St. Placide de Charlevoix
Chicoutimi	du Faubourg	St. Jean River
	du Lac Ha!Ha!	Des Ha!Ha! River
Compton	Drouin	Coaticook River
	Eustis	Massawippi River
	John Cook	Eaton River
	McDermott	N. Branch, Eaton River
	Fisher Hill	Riviere au Saumon
	Wellis Leggett	Eaton River
Drummond	Davitt/Monaghan	Drummondville
Gaspe Nord	Galipeault	Grande Vallee River
Gatineau	Marois (private)	Branch of Gatineau River
	Cousineau	Picanoc River
	l'Aigle	Desert River
	Wakefield/Meach Lake	Meach Brook
	Barry/Kelly	Stag Creek
	Savoyard	Gatineau River
Huntingdon	Powerscourt	Chateaugay River
Kamouraska	College/Ouelle	Ouelle River
Labelle	de Ferme Rouge	du Lievre River
	Armand Lach a lne	Kiamika River
	Meilleur	Kiamika River
	Chemin L'Annonclation	Macaza River
Laviolette	Ducharme	Bostonnais River
	Thiffault	Bostonnais River
L'Islet	du Sault	Grand Noire River
Lotbiniere	St. Andre	Filkars River
	Caron	du Chene River
Matane	Jean Chasse	Matane River
	Coulee Carrier	Matane River
	Belanger	Tartigou River
	Ti Pierre	Blanche River
	Francois Gagnon	Matane River
Matapedia	Heppell	Matapedia River
	Routhierville	Matapedia River
	Anse St. Jean	Matapedia River
Megantic	Reed Mill	Palmer River
	Lambert	Bulstrode River
Missisquoi	Guthrie	Groat Creek
	Freeport/Cowansville	Yamaska River
	Desrivieres	Aux Brochets River
Montcalm	Gareau (private)	du Lievre River
	Edwards Canadian Village	Red River
Montmagny	Ste. Lucie	NW Branch, Noire River
Nicolet	des Raymond	St. Wenceslas River
	Philemon Deschenes	St. Wenceslas River
Papineau	Bowman	du Lievre River
Pontiac	Marchand	Coulonge River
Rimouski	St. Anaclet	Neigette River
	des Draveurs	Petite Neigette River
	de la Riviere Hatee	Hatee River
	Beausejour	du Brule Brook
	Rouge	Rimouski River
Roberval	Rouge	Noire River
	Painchaud (private)	Ticouape River
Saguenay	Louis Gravel	Ste. Marguerite River
	Baie St. Ludger	St. Athanase Ouest River
St. Maurice	St. Mathieu	Shawinigan River
Shefford	Cousineau	Brandy Creek
Sherbrooke	Capleton	Massawippi River
	Milby	Moe River
Stanstead	Narrows	Fitch Bay Narrows
Temiscamingue	Landry	Fraser River
	La Loutre/E. Paquin	Loutre River
Temiscouata	St. Jean de la Lande	Baker Brook
Terrebonne	Prud'homme	du Diable River
Wolfe	St. Camille	Middle Branch, Nicolet River

EDITOR'S NOTE: Information for this directory of covered bridges came from booklets and travel guides submitted by Reiman Publications subscribers and from the *World Guide to Covered Bridges*, published by the National Society for the Preservation of Covered Bridges. See page 150 for the Society's address and for membership information.

YOU NEVER KNOW what adventure lies just around the bend when you go out searching for covered bridges on a sunny autumn day. Don Shenk, Millersville, Pennsylvania, took the photo.